The Soviet Industrial Worker

SOCIAL CLASS, EDUCATION AND CONTROL

The Soviet Industrial Worker

SOCIAL CLASS, EDUCATION AND CONTROL

David Lane and Felicity O'Dell

St. Martin's Press · New York

Contents

List of Tables and Figures

Acknowledgements

This book would not have materialised without the help of many people. Dr David Lee, of the University of Essex, prompted my interest in the training of industrial workers by suggesting that some research could usefully be conducted into this topic. The British Social Science Research Council supported Dr O'Dell as a research officer on a project out of which the present book grew. The Council also supported visits to the USSR by both authors to collect data. In Britain, the librarians at the University of Essex, and the Baykov Library at Birmingham University went to great lengths to provide us with materials. In the USSR we were particularly helped by the Leningrad branch of the Great Britain/USSR Society; and officials at the State Committee on Vocational and Technical Education dealt with many of our questions. When in the USSR much use was made of materials in the Leningrad Public Library and in the Lenin Library, Moscow. Our thanks go to Dr Christel Lane and Dr John Barber, who commented on the draft.

University of Cambridge,   *David Lane*
Social and Political Sciences Committee,   November 1977
Free School Lane,
Cambridge.

CHAPTER 1

The Evolution of the Soviet Industrial Working Class

Our general concern in this book is the place and role of the Soviet industrial worker in Soviet society. But we cannot consider all aspects of his life, and we shall concentrate on his class position and on the ways that education affects socialisation and social stratification. Four major problems are of concern. First is the contour of the boundaries of the working class in state socialist society and its form of political and social integration. Second is the way that technical competence in a modernising society is developed through the educational system and the way that occupation becomes a key to position in the stratification order. Third is the problem of making political reliability and support for the social order the prerogative of schools and other socialising media. The fourth problem concerns the stratification of occupational position — the definition of the preferability or status of occupations and their accessibility to various strata.

In this chapter we discuss the position of workers in the changing class and occupational structure, and in the second and third chapters we examine the worker in the context of the factory and his orienta- tion to work. In the chapters that follow, the education and socialisa- tion of the industrial worker are situated in the context of a rapidly developing society. We discuss the objectives of the Soviet state with regard to the socialisation of attitudes towards work and examine the demand by pupils for various kinds of educational institution and the popularity of different occupations. Finally, we deal with the implications of the occupational and educational structure for the system of social stratification. Throughout the book, we have as our main focus Soviet industrial workers: their class position, education, socialisation and control, ambition, attitude to work, and position in the stratification order.

A difficulty in this, as in all research on the Soviet Union conducted in the West, is that one must rely on data published in the USSR. Soviet researchers do not highlight conflict in their society, and

1

often seek to reinforce their society's legitimacy. We have, however, used Soviet data in our research. Soviet surveys serve to illustrate trends and bring out distinctions between various strata of workers. While acknowledging that an element of 'received ideology' is revealed in Soviet research, we believe that this is not sufficient to reject using it; 'ideology' is present in Western research, but does not invalidate its uses. As Hough has argued, 'Western observers have been so obsessed of the fear of being "taken in" by Soviet propaganda that they have too often based their judgements about the Soviet Union on the worst conceivable possibility, not the most probable' (Hough, 1976:12). Soviet data about the Soviet Union are used by some writers only to illustrate inadequacies of the system, and the uncritical acceptance of *émigré* and journalistic impressions about the Soviet Union has had an undue influence on the selection and framing of our knowledge about, and attitudes to, that country.

Our first task is to define the assumptions we make about the position of industrial workers in the Soviet class structure, to describe briefly the evolution of the working class and to indicate how it is located in the various structures making up contemporary Soviet society.

WORKERS IN THE CLASS STRUCTURE

The industrial worker holds an important place in Marxist thought and in the present structure of socialist societies. We would define manual industrial workers as a component part of the working class: they constitute that group of wage labourers who are employed in manual or semi-manual tasks in direct production in large-scale, technologically advanced and capital-intensive industry. Their labour process is characterised by a highly developed division of labour entailing specialisation of occupational roles; they are the kernel of 'productive' workers in the sense that their labour is embodied in a product that is objectified and exchanged — unlike most non-manual workers, whose work activity vanishes at the moment of production, though it is often indirectly embodied in a product. The produce of industrial workers is not directly owned by them, and what they produce is determined either by a market (under capitalism) or by a centrally organised bureaucratic structure (as in state socialist societies). Industrial workers play an important part in the socio-political sphere: under socialism, at least in theory, they play a part in the activity of 'leading society and production' — they are part of a class 'for itself' (Shkaratan, 1970:100). Manual (industrial) workers form a substantial part but not the only part of the working class, which we would define to include in the Soviet Union all manual and non-manual labour occupied in publicly owned institutions concerned with production, distribution and exchange. Of growing importance under conditions of advanced technology are highly qualified, technically trained, mainly non-manual workers whose activity we consider to be part of the industrial working class because such workers are an intrinsic part of the production process.

Before considering the changes that have taken place in the structure of the Soviet working class, some discussion of the orientation adopted and the terminology used by Soviet sociologists, on whom we have to rely for data, is necessary. The class division of the population into 'workers' and 'collective farmers' utilised by Soviet sociologists and philosophers is a rough and ready index for showing gross social changes and class divisions, but it includes many important sub-divisions. The working class, formed of all wage labourers employed in state institutions, is divided into manual and non-manual strata. The non-manual group includes all those employed by the state in industry, commerce, culture and public service: they perform mainly 'mental labour' rather than physical work. At present about three-quarters of this non-manual group may be classified as 'specialists' having some form of qualification and performing skilled non-manual work. The 'specialist' group may again be divided into those with engineering/technical skills having at least a specialised secondary education (usually referred to as ITRs, *inzhenerno— tekhnicheskie rabochie* — engineering and technical workers) and the intelligentsia proper — the latter stratum usually having higher education and performing the most creative cultural roles and those of administration and leadership. One cannot mechanically dichotomise these groups, as a stratum of engineers (technically ITRs) may fall into the latter group. In this book, however, our major concern is with the industrial worker as a social and economic category within the working class. (For discussions of different Soviet views see Shkaratan, 1970:112-30; *Rabochi klass...*, 1974:29 *et seq.*; Brodersen, 1966; Brown, 1966; Conquest, 1967.)

Collective farmers are in Soviet parlance a social class: their class membership is determined not by their occupation but by the fact that they live and work on a collective farm. The collective is a unit of co-operative production; it technically owns the seeds, livestock and equipment of the farms and it formally trades its produce with the Ministry of Agriculture and actually sells some produce on the free market; also collective farmers indulge in their own form of private agricultural production on their garden plots. Hence the category includes men and women in many different trades, such as drivers and clerks, and professions such as agronomists and librarians. The vast majority of collective farmers however live on and are engaged in unskilled manual work on the farm. In official statistics, 'manual' and 'non-manual workers' exclude collective farmers but include persons employed on state farms. (State farms are agricultural units organised like industrial enterprises: the employees are in direct employment by the government.)

In the view of Soviet writers, these groups are subject to a continual process of change. The creation of the material and technical base for the building of a communist society not only destroys the basis of hostile (antagonistic) class relationships but also leads to the decline and eventual elimination of collective forms of ownership and the withering away of the class of collective farmers. It should be noted here, however, that there is little sign of collective farms 'withering away' at present. Also, in theory, with changes in property class relations, the boundaries between formal class groups become insignificant and distinctions between manual and non-manual labour decline (*Rabochi klass . . .*, 1974:48,51): the rising level of technology reduces the number of manual jobs, the nature of production increasingly requires an admixture of manual and non-manual skills, and the new skills needed by the technological process are of a technical rather than a manual kind. In practice, however, while we shall see that some changes are taking place to reduce the distinction between manual and non-manual labour, the absolute (though not the relative) number of manual workers in recent years has increased.

In our view, non-manual workers in production enterprises are not, as assumed by Stalin and others, part of a separate stratum outside of the working class; they become an integral part of it. This is because in a Marxist sense their relationship to the means of production is the same as that of manual workers: all are wage-earners employed in state-owned enterprises; all contribute directly to production in the national economy; all to some degree share a similar political ideology. Technicians, craftsmen, skilled workers and engineers in production form the highly educated, socially aware and most politically active part of the working class. This distinguishes the political conjuncture of the Soviet working class from that under capitalism, where generally the industrial executives, directors and engineers (and also many technicians) have a class allegiance to the bourgeoisie, and where a stratified system of education, distinctive social background and political orientation reinforce class positions. Most Marxists would argue that in such a situation the growing numbers of scientific, technological, executive and administrative employees generally identify their subjective class interest with the ruling class. Hence, unlike writers such as Braverman (1974:12), we reject the view that the Soviet system of labour organisation is simply an 'imitation' of the Western capitalist model. The political context of the Soviet enterprise makes a Marxist-type of convergence model unrealistic (see Lane, 1977).

Positing these strata of technicians and engineers as part of the most politically advanced group is also not in line with the thinking of many orthodox Marxists, who emphasise the role of the manual worker in the production enterprise. It is true that before the revolution in Russia the most technically advanced sectors of the economy were in the metal fabrication industries, and thus Lenin regarded these workers as the most politically advanced and as the social basis for the overthrow of the system. In *The Development of Capitalism in Russia,* Lenin regarded the proletariat in the heavy machine industry as the 'vanguard' of the masses of workers and the oppressed (Lenin, 1958:586). This has given rise to forms of political utopianism on the part of some Marxists and socialists who still identify the development of class consciousness and the kernel of the working class with this stratum of manual workers. While it is undeniably true that manual workers in metal manufacture are part of the working class, it is disputable that they are always politically its leading component. Conditions have changed in the USSR (and in the West) economically and politically, and now there is a large stratum of the working class formed by technicians, engineers and skilled workers whose activity might be defined as 'non-manual'. The conditions of industry and the role played by the manual worker in pre-revolutionary Russian industry have been superseded by technological progress. In conditions of advanced capitalism, the *political* identification of some of these non-manual strata with the bourgeoisie has obscured their place in the working class, as defined by their relations to the means of production (Wright, 1976; cf. Poulantzas, 1975). Such obfuscation does not apply under conditions of state socialism, although it should not be overlooked that in the present conditions of state socialism one may detect differences of economistic interest and political commitment between various strata of workers: we do not wish to minimise such distinctions.

Engineering and technical workers in production enterprises may be distinguished from other strata of non-manual workers who are not at all or only indirectly connected with material production — employees in culture (theatre, mass media), employees of trade union and Party, officials in the Soviets, and professionals (such as lecturers and teachers). Such non-manual employees are concerned with reproducing the social relations to the means of production. In a sense, then, these persons may be said to be a social stratum having a specific cultural role rather than being simply a part of the working class. Under capitalism this stratum may be sharply divided socially from the working class; in politically unitary class societies such as the Soviet Union this class disjunction in a Marxist sense does not follow, though the narrower social, economic and political interests of this group do not always coincide with those of the industrial manual working class. Their position derived from the social division of labour defining specific occupational roles gives them certain privileges in political and social domains, which is not qualitatively the same thing as class domination.

While the simple categorisation of manual and non-manual workers in terms of the quality of their labour input becomes increasingly less relevant, other distinctions between various strata of the working class have more salience. It is certainly not the case that with the development of socialism the working class becomes a unitary and undifferentiated group. Social stratification arises from the social division of labour, which gives rise to an occupational structure. The division of work activity involves specialised and different social functions and qualitative differences between groups playing certain specified roles. The character of work performed and the place a worker has in the system of social production become of central importance (see also, Shkaratan, 1970:117, 130-44; Senyavski *et al.*, 1971, chapter 1). Also, different occupations develop cultural characteristics such as occupational languages and forms of solidarity, which help to create levels of status of a general social relevance (Osipov, 1975:42). Hence, the differentiation of occupation, educational background, financial rewards and culture become important influences in creating forms of stratification among the working class. As Gordon and Klopov have put it:

> in the workers' milieu, strata are being distinguished ever more distinctly which differ not ... by their relation ... to the means of production etc. but by their level of culture in the broad socio-logical sense of this term as a designation of the totality of life conditions, norms, traditions and knowledge directly determining man's behaviour .... [Cited in Yanowitch and Fisher, 1973:33]

Such forms of stratification are reflected in levels of expectations and ambitions, in patterns of consumption and in forms of participation by various groups in the political and economic processes of society.

One of the major characteristics of the Soviet working class, to which we shall now turn, has been its rapid structural change over time. This has included an increase in the share of manual and non-manual workers in the population, rapid urbanisation, the rise of women in paid employment, and an improving educational and technical level.

Macro Social Change

One of the most striking developments in the Soviet occupational structure has been the change in proportions of agricultural and manual and non-manual workers. In Soviet Russia in 1928 manual and non-manual workers (including members of families but excluding peasants) came to only 17.6 per cent of the population (manuals 12.4 per cent and non-manuals 5.2 per cent). By 1939 this group had risen to 50.2 per cent (33.2 per cent manual, 20 per cent non-manual); and by 1977 61.6 per cent of the population were manual and 22.7 per cent non-manual workers (*Narkhoz 1922-72*:35 and *Narkhoz za 60 let*:8). Total employment for manual and non-manual workers (excluding collective farmers) rose from 6.2 million in 1922 to 33.9 million in 1940, 40.4 million in 1950, 62.0 million in 1960 and reached 104.2 million in 1976. The total number of manual workers has risen more evenly than that of the non-manual group: in 1976 there were 72.9 million manual workers, a more than four-fold increase over the 1932 figures (17.8 million). By 1977 manual workers were the largest social group in the USSR, being almost three times the size of the non-manual group and nearly four times as great as the collective farmers.

These changes entailed a vast movement from village to town. In 1926 only 17 per cent of the population was urban; by 1940 the towns' share had risen to 33 per cent, i.e. from 27.6 million to 63.1 million (Arutyunyan, 1964:113). Between 1928 and 1935 some 17 million people left the countryside and settled in the towns (much larger numbers arrived and went back). By 1977 the urban population had grown to 159.6 million (62 per cent of the total) (*Narkhoz za 60 let*:7).

In addition, many urban women who previously were occupied in household duties or who were in domestic service entered the industrial workforce. In pre-revolutionary Russia 55 per cent of women in employment were in domestic service. From 1929, when 3.1 million women were in the workforce (27 per cent of the total), the number rose to 12 million (38 per cent) in 1940. The proportion in industry rose from 28.6 per cent in 1928 to 42.9 per cent in 1940. By 1975, 51 per cent of the workforce (52.5 million) was female: 90 per cent of able-bodied women of working age were in paid employment.

The peasant complexion of the industrial working class after the revolution may be gauged by the fact that at the Serp i Molot factory in Moscow the proportion of workers from peasant families was 50 per cent before 1917, 51 per cent in 1928, 55 per cent in 1929 and 69 per cent in 1930-1; 58 per cent of coal miners in 1918 came from peasant families, 71 per cent in 1928, and 79 per cent in 1930-1 (the last figure refers only to the major coal-mining area of the Donbass); of metal workers in Leningrad in 1926-7, 39 per cent were of peasant parents, and in 1929 the number rose to 44 per cent (Arutyunyan, 1964:115). This population movement took place against the background of collectivisation. Young men moved from country to town to form a young and inexperienced working class: the average age of workers in various occupations ranged from twenty-six to thirty-three years (Shkaratan, 1970:231).

The average rate of increase of numbers of workers in paid employment has tended to fall over time: between 1922 and 1940, it averaged 15.2 per cent per annum, from 1950 to 1955, 4.5 per cent and between 1970 and 1976 the average annual increase fell to 2.4 per cent. In addition, it must be borne in mind that the total population rose from 147 million in 1927 to 257.8 million in 1977. The population of the USSR increased at an average annual rate of 3.0 per cent between 1922 and 1940 and, after the net decrease of 15.6 million between 1940 and 1950, the rate of population increase has fallen from an annual average of 1.7 per cent between 1950 and 1955 to 0.9 per cent between 1970 and 1977. These facts serve to illustrate the rapid structural change that has taken place: a swift population growth, a movement of population from village to town, the creation of an urban working class with a recent peasant background.

Industrial growth and occupational change may be seen to have had different social effects in different periods. During the prewar period (1926−1939), the total number of non-manual workers (including those on collective farms) increased from 2.9 million to 13.8 million, an average rate of growth of 12.7 per cent per annum, and the share of non-manual workers (as a proportion of the total number of workers) rose from 25.2 per cent to 30 per cent. The average annual rate of growth of non-manual occupations has been at a much lower level after 1940: between 1939 and 1959 it averaged 0.6 per cent, and between 1959 and 1970 1.7 per cent. While the *rate of growth* of the non-manual group as a whole has declined, however, the absolute numbers of manual and non-manual workers alike have increased. Of the 10.2 million occupied in non-manual labour in 1940, specialists came to only 2.4 million; between 1960 and 1976 the number of non-manual workers rose from 16.1 million to 31.3 million, whereas the total number of employed specialists rose from 8.78 million to 24 million (*Narkhoz za 60 let*:477). Thus we can see from these figures that a most profound change had occurred between the prewar and the postwar period: in 1940 approximately a quarter of non-manuals were specialists; by 1976 the figure had risen to over three-quarters.

These changes are in addition to a general amelioration of the standards of education of the working class as a whole. In 1918, 21 per cent of men and 56 per cent of women employed in factories were illiterate (Rashin, 1961:12). By the 1930s, with the intensive increase in the numbers of workers in industry, the rates of illiteracy fell to 7.2 per cent in 1930 and to 3.6 per cent in 1934 (Rashin, 1961:13). The educational system raised the general educational standard of workers. Changes in the educational levels over generations are shown by data in Table 1.1, which is based on a survey of 10,720

TABLE 1.1 *Educational background of workers in Leningrad factories in 1963, by age*

Age (years)	To 4 classes	5—6 classes	7—9 classes	10—11 classes	Middle specialist	Incomplete higher
−18	1.0	12.2	73.0	12.3	1.3	—
18—20	1.0	8.8	58.5	29.5	2.0	0.2
21—25	1.3	10.1	54.3	27.0	6.1	1.2
26—30	7.3	21.2	49.2	15.1	5.2	2.0
31—40	15.0	30.0	45.0	5.9	3.6	0.5
41—50	28.6	21.4	37.3	6.4	4.2	2.1
50+	55.2	18.7	14.5	4.2	5.5	1.9

Source: Blyakhman *et al.* (1965:19).

Leningrad factory workers in 1963. A high proportion of the older generation had only primary education: of those over fifty, 55.2 per cent had up to four years' schooling. Of the younger age groups the overwhelming majority had had secondary education: in the 18—20 group, over 90 per cent had more than seven years. Similarly, at Uralmashzavod, in 1950 only 6.7 per cent of the workers had eight or more years of education, whereas in 1969 51.8 per cent were in this education group (Iovchuk and Kogan, 1972a:121). By 1970, 41 per cent of urban workers in the USSR had incomplete secondary education, and 23.3 per cent had secondary education or above; in 1959, by comparison, over half (56.8 per cent) of the workers had primary education or less, and only 10 per cent had complete secondary education or above (census data, cited in *Rabochi klass . . .,* 1974:79).

CHANGES IN OCCUPATIONAL STRUCTURE

These changes reflect a redistribution of labour between various sectors of the economy and the growth of certain occupations. In support of sociologists such as Treiman (1970) we believe that the Soviet *occupational* pattern substantially follows that of Western capitalist countries (cf. Garnsey, 1975 and Matthews, 1972:109). The more industrialised a society becomes, (i) the smaller the proportion of the labour force engaged in agriculture, and (ii) the higher the ratio of non-manual workers in the non-agricultural labour force (Treiman, 1970: 217).

TABLE 1.2 *Industrial distribution of the labour force*, Russia and the Soviet Union, selected years 1897-1976*

Industry	1897 (i)	1897 (ii)	1913	1926	1940	1950	1959	1964	1970	1976
(1) Agriculture	64	77	75	71	54	48	41	33	27	23
(2) Manufacturing and construction	18	10	9	14	23	27	32	35	37	38
(3) Transport and communications	2	2	2	4	5	5	6	8	8	9
(4) Trade	5+	4	9	3	5	5	5	6	7	8
(5) Public administration	1+	1	**	2	3	3	3	2	2	2
(6) Education and health	1+	1	1	4	6	8	10	13	15	16
(7) Other services	7	5	4	2	4	4	3	3	4	4
(8) A (row (1))	64	77	75	71	54	48	41	33	27	23
(9) M (rows (2) plus (3))	20	12	11	18	28	32	38	43	45	47
(10) S (rows (4) to (7))	16	11	14	11	18	20	21	24	28	30
(11) Total civilian labour force (rows (8) to (10))	100	100	100	100	100	100	100	100	100	100
(12) M/S ratio	1.2	1.1	0.8	1.6	1.6	1.6	1.8	1.8	1.6	1.56

* The definitions and coverage of the data for the various years are not entirely consistent. Figures for 1897 (col. i) one worker per family business: 1926 excludes all family workers and 1959 excludes workers on private plots, but both count all persons reported as workers in the censuses. At least for the later years, there seems to be little difference between "family workers" and "workers on private plots" (cf. 1959) . . . 1897 (col. ii) is based on the distribution of the total population and thus "favours" agriculture to the extent that rural families are larger than urban. It appears to conform with the definitions of later years better than 1897 (i). The figures for 1913, 1940, 1950, 1959, are based on annual full-time equivalents and include family workers also as full-time equivalents' (Ofer, 1973:187).

** Included in other services.

Sources: Ofer (1973:187); *Narkhoz 1972:*501; *Narkhoz za 60 let:*459

Figure 1.1   Changes in the distribution of the Soviet workforce throughout the main sectors of the economy, 1897-1976

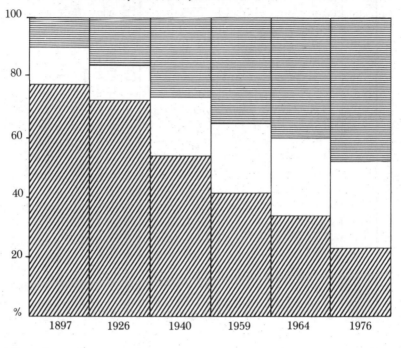

Sectors of employment:

 Agriculture

Manufacture and construction, transport and communications

Service

Based on: Ofer (1973:187); *Narkhoz za 60 let:*459

The data in Table 1.2 and Figure 1.1 show that the proportion engaged in agriculture has fallen dramatically from 75 per cent in 1913 to 54 per cent in 1940, 41 per cent in 1959 and 23 per cent in 1976.

Correspondingly, increases in employment have taken place in the areas of manufacturing and construction, transport and communications and education and health. The share of workers in manufacturing, building, transport and communications has risen from 11 per cent in 1913 to 47 per cent in 1976, and the share of workers engaged in the service industries has risen from 14 per cent to 30 per cent in the same period. While the service industries showed a very small increase in the pre-Second World War years (from 14 per cent in 1913 to 18 per cent in 1940), since 1950 they have increased by 50 per cent and far more rapidly than has manufacturing industry. Hence, comparing with other countries the relatively high proportion of workers in agriculture and the low share in the tertiary sectors diverts attention away from the dynamics of changes taking place. (Garnsey, 1975:442, gives a 'snapshot' of various countries and the USSR in 1959-60. Note that in Figure 1.1 we have bracketed together manufacture, construction, transport and communications whereas in Table 1.3 services include transport and communications.) While Garnsey notes that in 1959-60 'the proportion of the labour force employed outside agriculture and manufacturing is strikingly low from a comparative view', the trend is for the USSR to become more like advanced capitalist economies. This may be illustrated by juxtaposing the 1976 figures against those cited by Garnsey (see

TABLE 1.3 *Distribution of employment by economic sector in selected countries*

		Primary*	Sector Secondary**	Tertiary†
USSR	1960	39.0	32.0	29.0
France	1959-60	20.7	27.7	51.6
Italy	1959-60	29.4	26.9	43.7
USA	1959-60	7.3	25.9	66.8
Austria	1959-60	24.3	31.2	44.5
USSR	1976	23	38	39

*   Agriculture and forestry.
** Manufacture and construction.
† Transport, communication, trade, services, health, education, central and local government service, banking, insurance, domestic service.

Sources: Data for 1959-60 Garnsey (1975:442); USSR 1976, *Narkhoz za 60 let*:459.

Table 1.3). From this table we see that the structure of employment in the USSR in 1976 was much closer to that of Italy and Austria in 1959-60 than it was to the USA (or to the UK for that matter) in those years. Since 1940 there has been a tendency for the *proportion* of the workforce engaged in 'material production' to fall: in 1940 it constituted 88.3 per cent of the total, in 1953 84.7 per cent, in 1968 78.7 per cent and in 1976 75.4 per cent (Shkaratan, 1970:316 and *Narkhoz za 60 let*:460).

Scientific and technical advance has had important effects on the structure and functions of the working class. New technology, the introduction of new materials, mechanisation and the advent of computers have changed, at least to some extent, the character of labour within industry. It has been estimated for instance that 65.4 per cent of all new jobs arising since 1959 have been due to the growing complexity of equipment (Pliner and Inostrantsev, 1974:19). Automation is a particularly significant recent development influencing occupational structure: in 1971-74, 1504 automated systems were introduced compared with 414 in the preceding four years (*Narkhoz 1974*:152). The number of installed mechanised conveyor belts in industry rose from 42,947 in 1965 to 114,108 in 1975 (1 July) (*Narkhoz za 60 let*:150). And thus fewer manual and unskilled workers (proportionately, if not in absolute numbers) are required. Mechanisation has also enabled a smaller number of workers to maintain given levels of production in different branches of industry. In the chemical industry, for example, the value of production between 1940 and 1967 rose 19 times, whereas the number of workers rose only 3.4 times, and labour productivity rose by 671 per cent (data cited by Shkaratan, 1970:323). Overall in Soviet industry, in the period 1970-75, labour productivity rose by 6.0 per cent per annum (Chapman, 1977:41) and in 1976 it rose by 4 per cent (*SSSR v tsifrakh v 1976g*:28).

In the period 1959-69 there has been a 2.5 times increase of those watching automated processes (Shafranova, 1972:18) which has been paralleled by a relatively slow growth of workers doing manual jobs: those doing manual work not using machines or mechanical apparatus rose by 18 per cent (Shafranova, 1972:18). It is important to note also that the number of workers in absolute terms using and maintaining automated machinery is very small: in 1965 in machine-tools and metalworking, only 0.6 per cent; in the chemical industry 3 per cent (data cited in Shkaratan, 1970:324). In 1962, 44 per cent of the total number of workers were in manual work of one kind or another not using machinery (data cited in Matthews, 1972:115). But the decline in the proportion of manual workers becomes evident if a longer period of time is considered: between the censuses of 1959 and 1970, the proportion of the urban employed population in mainly manual work fell from 78.9 per cent to 67.9 per cent (*Itogi vsesoyuznoy perepisi* . . . vol. 6, 1973:7), although, as pointed out above, their absolute numbers increased.

Automation has reduced the need for workers to do routine manual jobs only in a relatively small number of factories, however, and the demand for manual workers continues. This is probably due to the fact that Soviet industry has expanded both *extensively* and *intensively*. In the advanced Western countries, the decline in the proportion of manual workers is accounted for by greater intensive development of technology; in the USSR, however, the country is at a relatively lower technological level, so extensive and intensive industrialisation take place in parallel, rather than in sequence. Besides intensive growth owing to increases in labour productivity and in the output-to-capital ratio, extensive growth owing to increases in the factors of production has also occurred. In the Urals, where the proportion of manual workers in the employed population rose from 62.5 per cent in 1959 to 66.4 per cent in 1970, *intensive* growth took place, but in such places as Byelorussia, where the share of workers in the labour force rose from 33.2 per cent to 54.0 per cent between these dates, *extensive* growth was responsible (data from *Rabochi klass...*, 1974:65-7). In the less industrialised regions an inflow of population came from the countryside, whereas in the more industrialised areas labour recruitment was from within the working class and increases in production resulted from the higher level of productivity of workers and from the growth of capital. We see no reason to doubt that occupational structure is closely linked to technological advance and that views advanced to the effect that 'The Soviet government exercises an unprecedented prerogative in influencing the structure of the labour force . . .' (Matthews, 1972:109) in fact amount to little more than saying that the government takes decisions about levels of growth, investment and employment: the actual *structure* of the labour force is largely determined by the kind and level of technology, and the socially accepted ways of manning. It is in the context of similarities in the division of labour that the organisation of the work process in the USSR has parallels with the capitalist West

(Braverman 1974:14, 23-4).

The general level of skill has increased, as may be seen by examination of Table 1.4. In 1961, the lowest level of skill accounted for 22.4 per cent of workers in machine-tools and metalworking,

TABLE 1.4 *Distribution of workers in machine-tools and metalworking industries in the USSR by grades of skill, 1961 and 1972*

Year	Grade of skill					
	1	2	3	4	5	6
1961	22.4	29.5	24.5	15.2	6.9	1.5
1972	10.3	25.5	26.1	19.8	13.8	4.5

Source: Rabochi klass . . . (1974:82)

whereas in 1972 it came to 10.3 per cent. In 1961 only 1.5 per cent of the workers were in the highest grade of skill (6), whereas in 1972 4.5 per cent were in this grade. These figures, however, must not only be taken at their face level, for it is also possible that changes in the definition of jobs have taken place; such workers may be effectively paid more simply by redefining their jobs. The numbers of engineering and technical employees (ITRs) have grown substantially in all branches of industry: total numbers have risen from 4,045,000 in 1959 to 8,449,900 in 1970, and the number of employed engineers rose from 699,700 to 2,492,600 (*Itogi vsesoyuznoy perepisi . . .*, vol. 6, 1973:21).

Just as mechanisation and automation are leading to an increase in the proportion of workers who use machines and in the numbers of engineering and technical employees, so also is the amount of workers' time primarily devoted to 'mental work' increasing. This is not only because watching automated systems is mental work, but also because installing and maintaining these complex systems requires intellectual activity rather than physical effort. An adjuster of an automated line spends on average 52.1 per cent of his working time in observing the process of his machines, and another 26 per cent of his time on fitting and quality control, both of which involve little physical effort (Krevnevich, 1971:144).

Let us now turn to consider Treiman's hypothesis concerning the ratio between manual and non-manual workers. In broad occupational terms, the share employed primarily in non-manual jobs has risen from 19.5 per cent of the workforce in 1959 to 27.3 per cent in 1970 and the share in manual work has declined accordingly. (In freight transport, for instance, the percentage of workers occupied in manual work has fallen from 90.8 per cent in 1925 to 50.8 per cent in 1962: Shkaratan, 1970:33.) While one must concede that lower-grade white-collar workers constitute a smaller share of the labour force than in the West, these groups are growing in size. The number of typists and stenographers rose from 82,673 to 145,732 between 1959 and 1970; the number of secretaries and clerical workers rose from 233,388 to 355,357 (*Itogi vsesoyuznoy...*, vol. 6, 1973:33). Statistics show that the number of manual jobs has increased by 4 per cent over the period, whereas the corresponding increase in non-manual jobs has been 62 per cent (the overall increase in the occupied population was 16 per cent).

The number of employed 'administrative' workers defined in Soviet statistics is low by Western standards (Garnsey, 1975:446-9). But Komarov (1969), noting the high proportion of salaried employees in the USSR compared to the USA, goes on to point out that this difference is

> largely a consequence of the artificial limitation of the number of salaried workers *when their functions were handed over* to ITRS [engineering and technical workers]. . . . In addition, ITRs should be completely relieved of office work (writing letters, orders, reports, etc), [these] jobs should be handed over to the appropriate office worker.

A study of the working day of ITRs at several industrial enterprises showed that technological functions and scientific work came to 32.5−38 per cent of the total time (including unproductive and lost time, e.g. dinner breaks, etc), while administrative work and work with documents came to 29−34 per cent of the time (Mangunov, 1973:81).

Hence one should not be too much influenced by the classification of occupations, but should also consider the functions of the particular worker and the extent to which given roles are being efficiently performed. We feel justified in arguing that the tendency of the occupational structure is similar to that in the West: a decline in the number of manual workers employed in relation to the numbers of non-manuals. The major determinant of this movement is to be found in the changing levels of technology. Increasing mechanisation and the introduction of automation to Soviet industry throughout the sixties and seventies has thus affected the occupational structure in several important and intertwined ways. It has released workers for the non-productive sphere while enabling productivity to be increased. It has reduced the proportion of workers employed in manual labour while increasing the numbers of those using machines, especially of those involved in the repair of machines, and it has increased the proportion of those doing predominantly mental work. Here, then, we confirm the hypothesis that the greater the development of industrialisation, the higher is the ratio of non-manual to manual workers in the non-agricultural sector (Treiman, 1970:217).

Political and ideological 'considerations', to use Garnsey's terms, have shaped the trajectory and speed of industrial change, but in our view the occupational structure has evolved in a way not unlike that of capitalist societies. The small service sector and the low proportion of employees in clerical occupations should not be allowed to obscure this fact. These changes in the size of the industrial and occupational structure have required the adaptation of the educational system to provide for the training of industrial workers. In our view greater attention should be paid, not to the structure of occupations, but to forms of socialisation and patterns of recruitment, and to the political context in which the Soviet worker is situated.

THE POLITICAL ENVIRONMENT OF THE SOVIET WORKER

We would point to four major differences in the political context in which the Soviet worker finds himself, compared with his counterpart in the capitalist West. First, it is worth emphasising that the *class* structure (in a Marxist sense) and the political culture of the Soviet Union differentiates the Soviet worker from his fellow worker under capitalism. The Soviet industrial worker inherits a long revolutionary tradition reinforced by the cultivation of myths about it. Also workers have had considerable direct participation in the dominant political party. Even before the October Revolution, the urban industrial working class formed the mass base of the Bolshevik Party (Lane, 1969:21). Following the October Revolution, the proportion of manual workers in the Party fell, until in 1924 they came to only a quarter of the total membership. The Lenin enrolment in that year led to mass recruitment to the Party until in 1927 manual workers constituted 44 per cent (see *Kommunist* 1967, no. 15). The proportion of manual workers in the Party rose from 32 per cent in 1956, to 33.9 per cent in 1961, 40.5 per cent in 1972 and 42.0 per cent in 1977 (*Partiya i rabochi klass . . .,* 1973:36; *Partiinaya zhizn'* No. 21, 1977:28). Since 1960, the proportion of manual worker *entrants* to the Party has risen: between 1962 and 1965 it was 44.7 per cent, 1966-70 52 per cent, 1971-75 57.6 per cent and in 1976 was 58.6 per cent. The respective numbers for specialists (ITRs, scientific workers, agricultural specialists, teachers, doctors) were: 28.2 per cent, 26.4 per cent, 24.5 per cent, 25.1 per cent (*Partiinaya zhizn'* No. 21, 1977:25). In 1969 every tenth manual worker was in the CPSU, as was every third engineer, every second agronomist or animal specialist (*zootekhnik*), every fourth teacher and every fifth doctor (*Partiya i rabochi klass . . .,* 1973:33-4, 86). In the large industrial centres of Moscow, Leningrad, Sverdlovsk, the Don and Karaganda between 60 and 70 per cent of new members of the Party admitted since the XXIII Congress in 1966 have been manual workers (*Partiya i rabochi klass . . .,* 1973:37). In view of these facts one cannot lightly assume that the Party is 'cut off' from the manual working class. (Whether the working class is cut off from those who make the decisions is another matter.)

Second, membership of the Party must also be seen in the context of trade unions. In pre-revolutionary Russia the trade union movement as an independent wage-bargaining force was extremely weak. The incipient formation of stratification by occupational groups along trade union lines, as in Western society, was cut short and the trade union movement, as an autonomous force, was crushed in the early years of Soviet power (see Conquest, 1967: chapter 5). The trade unions formed on an industrial basis have become agents for integration of the working class into an industrial society. Western trade unions inherited much of the struggle for *civil* rights (to vote, to combine) not given to the working class in the transition from feudalism to capitalism; Soviet unions have developed in quite a different context — one in which the legal and constitutional rights of the worker have been secured by the dominant socialist party; and the concept of individual rights stemming from bourgeois society has remained relatively undeveloped. It is precisely because Soviet trade unions do not 'represent' the interests of specific groups of workers that they have contributed to the political homogenisation of the work force.

Third, the momentous happenings of the revolution, the civil war and collectivisation all helped to create feelings of strong political solidarity among the core of industrial workers who manned Soviet industry before the First Five-Year Plan in 1928, though this group was diluted both by casualties in the civil war and, more importantly, by the influx of peasants, especially with the advent of the great industrialisation drives. As a result the Soviet working class has developed with a large cultural component derived from the traditional Russian peasantry. (Very few rich peasants or dispossessed members of the bourgeoisie entered production on the shop floor: see Shkaratan, 1970:241-5, 257-9, 268-70. This had both social and political effects.) In 1918, for instance, 36 per cent of industrial workers were illiterate and ten-year education was introduced in the USSR only in 1970. As we noted above, it is only in the last twenty-five years or so that the educational level of the working class has reached that of the advanced West. Labour productivity has been lower than in the West and various campaigns ranging from Stakhanovism in the 1930s to societies of 'rationalisers and inventors' (VOIR) have been devised to improve the motivation and performance of Soviet workers, to overcome the slower pace and more careless style of work of the traditional peasant. This cultural artefact, we would argue, is responsible for low levels of productivity and craftsmanship, rather than political contradictions predicated on the political structure as suggested by Ticktin (1976:35).

The fourth major difference in the political situation of the Soviet worker compared with his Western counterpart is that for fifty years he has been employed in nationalised industry: by 1920, 88 per cent of workers in Russian industry were employed in nationalised factories; by 1935 only 10,000 workers were in factories in private ownership and nearly 25 million were in the state sector. Thus for over forty years there has been no possibility for the worker or his children to form or to aspire to own his own business. There is no process of an economic market which, as under capitalism, to quote Habermas, 'secures for the owners of the means of production the power, sanctioned in civil law, to appropriate surplus value and to use it privately and autonomously'. (Habermas 1976:26.) Structural unemployment is unknown to the contemporary Soviet working class. The rise of an 'aristocracy' of certain occupational groups of workers (such as printers) through *market* and trade union bargaining has been circumscribed by the Soviet state (though certain industrial groups, such as miners, are advantaged). Given the high rates of growth, managers and executives in industry have largely originated from within the working class. While we shall show that stratification by occupation and education is important, the Soviet working class has a greater unity between manual and non-manual, between managers and workers, between trade union and Party, than is the case in Western states. This greater homogeneity of the working class and its effective incorporation in Soviet society is furthered by the structural arrangements in the Soviet factory, which is the concern of the next chapter.

CHAPTER 2

The Worker in the Industrial Enterprise

The organisation of the Soviet factory differs in many respects from that of the Western capitalist firm. There are three significant institutions shaping the worker's life there: the factory administration, the Party organisation and the trade union. These institutions do not exist in isolation from each other with rigidly defined spheres of influence; in many areas they overlap. Ultimately, all the organisations are subordinate to the top *policy* decisions of the Party which explicitly seeks to use management, trade union and Party groups as support for its work. There are also various voluntary groups or commissions organised under the Party and unions and they carry out what is termed 'people's control'. Such groups attempt to prevent abuse by the administration and they also try to prevent infringements of discipline by the workers. Hence 'control' is seen in the context of the laws (*zakonomernosti*) governing the evolution of Soviet society, rather than the representation or safeguarding of the interests of specific groups. Let us briefly describe these institutions in the Soviet industrial enterprise. (On the administration of a technical trade school, see Appendix A.)

THE FACTORY ADMINISTRATION

The head of the factory administration is the director, who is responsible to a ministry, which in turn is subordinate to a Council of Ministers (this may be of a republic or of the USSR). The major task of the enterprise director is to fulfil (or over-fulfil) the economic plan for the enterprise. This is the major constraint on all factory employees and is the prime criterion of a factory's operating efficiency. All organisations in the factory, including the trade

22

unions, see their major task as helping to carry out the plan.

At the lower levels of authority in particular the emphasis is more on duties and responsibilities than on rights and privileges. The responsibilities of the brigade-leader are to ensure that his workers produce as much as possible, that they are punctual, that they are reprimanded for infractions of discipline and that the work produced is of a high quality. This latter demand is being especially strongly emphasised in the 1970s. Supervision of brigade-leaders is carried out by their immediate superiors who are in charge of whole sections or workshops.

In most factories there seems to be some direct contact between top-level management and the shopfloor workers. The factory director is encouraged regularly to go round his factory in order to talk to the workers and to receive their complaints (on a textile factory see Anisimova, 1971:44). Permanent production conferences (*postoyanno-deystvuyushchie proizvodstvennye soveshchaniya:* PDPS) also provide a regular flow of information between administration and workers. Members participate for one year and carry on discussions of the plans, output, norm-setting, safety precautions and other matters relating directly to production. Usually over half the participants are workers (information received in an interview with the head of Leningrad Central Trade Union School). The workers who take part in these conferences are selected by their trade union organisation. A study of twenty-one factories in the lathe-building industry showed that 42.4 per cent of their members were also Party members (Mukhachev and Borovik, 1975:33-4).

The Party in the Industrial Enterprise

An important feature of the life of the Soviet factory administration is that it is subject to 'control' (or checking) from the Party and other institutions, such as trade unions and various commissions organised by the Party and union. These bodies help to mobilise the masses, supervise the fulfilment of the plan and help with the education and recruitment of all personnel in the enterprise. Such 'control' is oriented to carrying out government directives and should not be confused with the location of an alternative source of legitimate power, as in the British sense of 'workers' control'. Such control is exercised through the party branch and through various bodies of

People's Control responsible to the Council of Ministers and usually organised by the unions.

As far as supervision of management is concerned, the party organisations at the factory have an explicit brief to:

> check the work of their enterprise;
> hear reports from the management and encourage a heightened sense of management responsibility for the tasks it has been set;
> create various commissions to study the state of affairs in the factory collective;
> request for checking any documents relevant to the efficient running of the factory from the management;
> make proposals and recommendations concerning the carrying out of measures required by Party directives;
> and to raise questions concerning factory management before higher Party and economic organs.
> [Taukin and Novikov, 1974:13-14. This reference is a brochure for Party activists, entitled 'Control of the Activity of the Administration'.]

In order to carry out such work thoroughly it is stressed that party members should be active in all the activities of the factory (Taukin and Novikov, 1974:15). At open party meetings, attended by both workers and management, accounts are given of the fulfilment of decisions: one account of a meeting at the Stroymekhanizatsiya factory at Krasnoyarsk reports that, though some suggestions were carried out, others remained 'on paper' (*Partiya i rabochi klass . . .,* 1973:135). The 'control' should be as extensive as possible and the party organisation is given access to all documents to help in its supervisory work. It is urged to take account not only of official reports but also of speeches made by workers at meetings and of letters and proposals that may have been written to the management.

A significant indicator of party control is that the appointment of directors usually has to be ratified by the party committee (Kulagin, 1974b:161). All those who hold a position of authority in the factory are subject to similar control. An Attestation Committee is formed of party, Komsomol (Young Communist League) and trade union representatives. References are obtained from the individual's previous superior and, when appropriate, his party and trade union branch. The Commission takes into account his contribution to the fulfilment of the state plans, his application of new techniques, his observance of state and factory discipline, his qualifications, his participation in socialist emulation competitions and his activities in political and social organisations. According to the attestation, managers may be removed from office, transferred or rewarded for any successes (Zhuravlev and Gol'din, 1976:69-70). Similarly, the party organisation keeps a list of people suitable for promotion to administrative positions (on the Belotserkovsk combine, see Ivashkevich, 1975:11).

This extensiveness of party rights and duties in connection with supervising management might imply that the factory director's position is being undermined by zealous activists. Many party commentators, however, emphasise that party organisations must not allow 'the slightest interference or usurping of management functions'. The principle of one-man management must be firmly supported (Taukin and Novikov, 1974:17). In practice, procedure varies from party secretaries colluding with the management to showing excess zeal in performing their function of 'control'. We agree with Andrle's general conclusions that, in practice, the party secretary's power is limited (Andrle, 1975:89-90). But contacts through the party organisation may prove to be very useful for the factory management in procuring resources. Andrle found only two cases where an ambitious factory party secretary tried to advance his own career by asserting a 'party interest' against the director (Andrle, 1975:104).

All the institutional structures discussed in this chapter play their part in the tasks of improving productivity and encouraging the desired attitudes to work among many workers. It is through the administrative structure of a factory that many Soviet campaigns are promoted — with the Party and trade union supporting and often initiating them.

One of the principles of Soviet ideology is the concept of worker participation in the running of society, and the Soviet authorities would claim that this principle is put into practice in the Soviet factory. The 'pay-off' of such participation is in increased production. A managing director of the large Leningrad Sverdlov machine-tools factory points out that workers are happier and have higher levels of job satisfaction when they feel that they have a say in decision-making (Kulagin, 1974a:120). In his factory no master-craftsman, foreman or manager is appointed without prior discussion with the workforce (either in mass or through their representatives). In his opinion this process should be taken a stage further, so that workers themselves either choose their new leaders or select them from a list prepared by the administration. This, it is argued, would heighten the worker's sense of responsibility towards his factory (Kulagin, 1974b:16).

As the Party legitimates itself as a workers' party, the role of the Party in the enterprise is of crucial importance. In 1976 41.6 per cent of party members were manual workers, and between 1971 and 1975 57.6 per cent of entrants to the Party were from this group. In addition, 17.6 per cent of party members are engineering and technical workers (*Partiinaya zhizn'*, No. 10, 1976:14-15). At the base of the party structure are the primary organisations and on 1 January 1976 there were over 390,000 such groups in the USSR, a quarter of which were in industrial enterprises, transport, communications and buildings (*Partiinaya zhizn'*, No. 10, 1976:18). In the early 1970s the average size of a primary organisation in an industrial enterprise was 89 Communists; at a construction site the average number was 39 members and at a *kolkhoz*, 49 (Taukin and Novikov, 1974:3-4). In large factories there will often be several such primary organisations, one for each major shop or department.

Party membership varies with the nature of the work done by the workers in question. Membership is low among unqualified workers, rising to higher proportions among more qualified groups and to as high as 54 per cent of management. The most ambitious and generally active workers seek to join the Party, and the Party itself is anxious to recruit members who may act as 'opinion-leaders'. In many large factories more than half of the members of the factory party committee are manual workers (*Partiya i rabochi klass . . .*, 1973:123, 134).

The Party plays an important guiding role in political and moral education at the factory in ways that are both direct and indirect. Meetings are called by the party organisations at the factory to present the communist attitude towards current issues and to encourage workers to participate in various types of campaigns. At such meetings the Party is able to gauge the responses of workers to party and government policy. Political 'inputs' are fed into the political system. Where the factory party organisation is working effectively it will 'take account of the critical remarks of workers'. At these meetings general problems of production, discipline and factory conditions are discussed, and they are attended by the management who may be called upon to account for action taken at previous meetings (*Partiya i rabochi klass . . .,* 1973:135, 139). Courses are organised on Marxism-Leninism, social science, economics and administration. In a slightly less direct way the Party is concerned with discipline, with helping the promotion of socialist 'traditions' and with mobilising workers towards whichever campaign is currently under way. All the measures carried out by the primary party organisation are in some way linked to the political education or 'socialisation' of workers. The Party also encourages activists to take a responsible part in life outside the factory, including street patrols (see Rozanov, 1965:503).

Party control over the life of an industrial enterprise is often defined in 'social development plans', which have been drawn up by many factories. These plans do not limit themselves to economic indicators but also concern themselves with 'human' factors. These include increasing mechanisation and automation, raising the technical level of production, improving labour conditions and methods of production and social welfare and improving the socio-cultural level of workers (Lozarev and Kazakova, 1971:4). Party influence in preparing these programmes is reflected in the fact that when the Dvigatel' factory in Estonia decided to draw up a social development plan for itself, it was the plant's party committee that selected the group of workers who were to compose the plan. The majority of the planners chosen were themselves party members.

The strength that party involvement can bring to such a project is its contacts with all areas of Soviet life and its ability to mobilise help wherever needed to implement plans as fully as possible. The plan that the Dvigatel' factory committee prepared also had social and occupational components. It had three sections, which included the reform of the occupational structure of the factory resulting from technical progress, the improvement of the material, educational and socio-cultural levels of the workers, and sociological research leading to the development of measures to form desired attitudes towards work and the collective. The final section covered the formation of attitudes outside the collective with a view to the eventual improvement of the factory itself. For example, the factory always had too few workers in certain basic trades like joiners, metal-workers and fitters, and so it was decided to encourage local school-children to have a more positive attitude towards such work with the hope that they would eventually themselves make a conscious and enthusiastic choice to become fitters or metal-workers (see Lozarev and Kazakova, 1971:4-10).

Another example of the extensiveness of party influence in the life of the industrial enterprise is given by the way in which cadres were found for a new tyre and rubber — asbestos combine in the Ukraine. Directors were appointed in 1964. In the late sixties the process of appointing other qualified specialists for the combine began. All those who expressed interest in work there were screened not just for their work record but also for their political qualities. They were interviewed by the specialists previously appointed, along with the secretary of the local Party (Ivashkevich, 1975:3-7). In this way the Party checked that those who were politically active were appointed to top positions in the new combine. The local party organisation also participated in the enlistment of workers at lower levels. In 1974-75 as many as one-sixth of those working at the Belotserkovsk combine were party members. A more typical proportion is at the Skorokhod footwear factory in Leningrad where in 1965, out of 11,322 workers, approximately 1000 (8.8 per cent) were party members and 1300 (11.5 per cent) were in the Komsomol (Ershova, 1969:541).

Other bodies through which the Party exerts influence are the various commissions on matters connected with the work of the factory. The general aim here is to increase the activity of the workers. The subjects of the commissions vary from fulfilment of state requirements to quality control and from the introduction of new technology to meeting export needs. Serving on them is con-sidered helpful to party members by giving them experience and the chance to influence certain aspects of the factory's work. In Leningrad alone in 1975 there were 887 factory commissions sitting on various topics and run by primary party factory organisations often in conjunction with the unions. Many are concerned with quality control and the introduction of new techniques. It is stressed that the work of the commissions is not simply to criticise and expose weaknesses (implying that in practice this is sometimes the case) but also to make positive suggestions (Taukin and Novikov, 1974:44-6).

Groups of the Young Communist League (the Komsomol) exist in all factories where there are young workers. The role of the

Komsomol on the shop floor is that of a kind of junior party movement, supporting party work wherever possible and serving as a training ground for future party activists. To this end, Komsomol members at the factory are singled out as being particularly suitable for holding 'tutoring' responsibilities — giving practical and moral guidance to young workers newly arrived on production. The factory Komsomol group also organises socialist emulation competitions and ceremonies.

THE UNION BRANCH

The third major institution in the Soviet industrial enterprise is the trade union. We see trade unions as having two major functions to perform in modern industrial societies. First, the union is an institution that integrates workers into the factory and the wider society. Second, it is a channel of dissension, representing the interests of workers *against* management in the system of industrial relations. Western trade unions, at least ostensibly, are concerned mainly with the second function and particularly with the defence of workers' wages. Increasingly, however, they do negotiate with governments and participate in 'social contracts' having wider implications — for the control of wage and price levels, and for productivity deals. Soviet unions are almost overwhelmingly concerned with the first function: they attempt to incorporate the worker into factory and social life and see themselves as an important part of the social compact between political party, government and industrial enterprise.

The Soviet unions still perform many of the activities that were carried out by unions in Western Europe in their formative years, by providing sickness, welfare and sporting activities; they also administer housing. Such provisions are now on a vast scale. In 1972 the unions controlled 94,000 clubs, houses of culture and cinemas; in twenty-nine sports organisations were more than 200,000 stadiums, sports halls and other sports facilities (*Partiya i rabochi klass . . .,* 1973:87). The union deals with housing and recreational facilities and kindergartens for workers' children. It administers sickness and other benefits when a worker is absent through illness or is incapacitated. Such administration is performed on a voluntary basis by union activists. This saves a great deal of money, but problems of social administration are now extremely complex and some observers feel that voluntary workers perform inefficiently and often arbitrarily. The point we would stress is that such voluntary administration has a positive effect on social integration at the work place. The Soviet *kollektiv* attempts to create a firm set of *gemeinschaft* relationships between its members. This may also be appropriate in providing 'informal' social welfare for a labour force recently uprooted from the countryside and having no family or other support in the town.

The trade union plays a leading part in the social activities of the production *kollektiv*. Compared with life in the West, life is more centred on the place of work in the USSR; there is a greater interlocking of social life and economic activity. The factory provides housing, social insurance, clubs and informal social activities. In one Moscow factory visited by the authors, between 70 and 80 per cent of the workers were in flats built by the enterprise. A study of the activity of work brigades in several factories in Sverdlovsk showed that their members meet socially outside work hours slightly more than once in every two weeks. Symphony concerts were attended by 6—11 per cent of members, art exhibitions by 22—31 per cent, lectures, talks and discussions by 25—47 per cent, theatres by 6—9 per cent and museums and exhibitions by 11—16 per cent (Iovchuk and Kogan, 1972a:87-8). The authors of this study also found that 27 per cent of the workers had their best friend in the same production brigade (Iovchuk and Kogan, 1972a:90-91). Even critical Soviet immigrants to Israel recall the integrative effects of the work place: 'I miss the collective where I work, where they respect me' (Gitelman, 1977:554).

A brief account of the work of the smallest trade union unit, the workshop branch, will serve to give a picture of the ways in which the ordinary worker is affected by trade union activity. A workshop branch may be typified by that in weaving workshop no. 1 at the Gus'-Khrustal'ny textile combine in Vladimir region; it consists of twenty-eight members from four different work brigades. There are four party members in the branch (*Opyt raboty profsoyuznoy . . .*, 1970:3-4). Its work is organised according to monthly plans that cover all the basic areas of its activity — mass production work, insurance, culture, safety precautions and physical culture.

Mass production work involves helping under-achievers to become more efficient (*Opyt raboty profsoyuznoy . . .*, 1970:8-9). It also includes keeping a daily record of each individual's performance and a monthly one of the productivity of each brigade (Anisimova, 1971: 12-15). In the light of these records each worker is given advice on the sort of training he should pursue to raise his qualifications, some being directed into 48-hour 'special purpose' courses and some into more detailed 120-hour production—technical courses. Occasionally the trade union will provide funds for a worker to attend a higher educational institution. The progress of the members engaged in study is closely observed by the trade union group, which listens to their reports, praising or reprimanding as appropriate (Anisimova, 1971:25).

The 'insurance' aspect of the work of the union branch deals with health facilities and various benefits. Of the twenty-eight members of the branch described above, seventeen spent some time during 1969 at a trade union rest home, sanatorium or prophylactic centre. During periods of sickness, the trade union arranges visits by union members to sick members.

The cultural side of the branch's work covers the organisation of lectures and discussions, a group subscription to the newspapers *Trud* (Labour) and *Sovetskie profsoyuzy* (Soviet Trade Unions) and the arrangement of festivities to mark a member's retirement and of congratulatory messages for members' birthdays, weddings and childbirths (*Opyt raboty profsoyuznoy . . .*, 1970: 10-11). There is one person in the branch with a particular responsibility for culture. Among other things he should arrange a programme of leisure activities for the members. In the branch described above it was found that many members choose to spend some of their free time, as well as their working time, together. Through cultural and social programmes, it is hoped to improve overall labour discipline. A trade union branch leader writes: 'socialist labour discipline is indissolubly linked not only to a person's work but also to his everyday life, his private life. And the trade union branch leader should never forget this' (Anisimova, 1971:42). Poor discipline in one's private life is felt to be reflected in unsatisfactory work performance — as is very clearly the case where alcohol is concerned — and a programme of leisure activities is considered to pay dividends in productivity. The branch leader is, therefore, concerned with both knowing about and 'improving' the private lives of branch members.

Ensuring that safety regulations are observed and providing sports facilities are the remaining two major areas of the typical branch's work. If safety precautions are not being maintained by the management, the trade union has the right to take action to reprimand the director. We may note here that there is a potential for conflict between the function of encouraging productivity and that of maintaining safety. It seems likely that in many cases the needs of production and productivity will take priority (see Ruble, 1977, for examples). Therefore, complaints about high norms and industrial accidents may not be resolved to the liking of aggrieved workers. This is the root of the grievances made to the Western press pleading for more 'independent' trade unions (Levin, 1977. *The Times* 27 January 1978. On Klebanov's group see *Labour Focus . . .*, 1978:2-7).

The work of even the smallest union branch is, therefore, quite extensive. A general meeting should take place at least once a month, at which competition results are read out, the quality of production is discussed and, when appropriate, any infractions of discipline since the last meeting are publicly condemned. If considered necessary, additional sanctions may be enforced — often in the form of deprivation of trade union privileges like holiday passes or of being put lower in the queue for factory housing. Decisions are taken as to how to mark the Lenin anniversary and so on.

Moral pressure, combined with access to facilities and help provided by the trade unions through insurance schemes, all help explain why 113.5 million workers or over 99 per cent of all white-collar and manual workers join a union (*Narkhoz za 60 let:* 90). Organisationally, Soviet unions are of the industrial type and include all the employees (except health staff) of an enterprise. Members pay dues of 1 per cent of their earned income.

Participation at the enterprise

The trade unions are also concerned with activating the workforce. One example of their work here is the organisation of 'communist *subbotniks*'. The *subbotniks* are Saturdays when people are encouraged to do their normal work without pay. In 1973 132 million people took part in the annual events of celebrating Lenin's birthday (*Profsoyuzy SSSR*, 1974: 401). This participation, however, is now more symbolic than economically motivated as in the earlier years of Soviet power. The trade union branch supports the 'rationalisation' work organised by the Party and the inter-brigade competitions arranged by the factory management. These kinds of activities date back to the Stakhanovite movement which began in 1935. Stakhanov was a leading record-breaker of productivity norms. The aim of the movement was to break down old technical norms and to improve labour activity to the level of the advanced capitalist countries. Many Stakhanovites were recent immigrants to the town from the country. It has been estimated that by 1939 40−47 per cent of workers participated in this form of activity (Lebedeva and Shkaratan, 1966:140). Another aspect of the work of the Stakhanovites that has had less publicity in the West is the movement to improve qualifications of workers: in December 1935, for example, out of a group of 250 Stakhanovites, 209 passed technical tests.

Nowadays, various commissions and groups are organised at the place of work to improve productivity and to encourage the participation of workers in social affairs. These include production conferences, technical councils and scientific and technical groups. In 1973 the Society for Scientific and Technical Activity (NTO) had branches in 100,000 factories and 6 million members (*Partiya i rabochi klass . . .,* 1973:147).

The All-Union Society of Inventors and Rationalisers (VOIR) was founded in 1958, and by 1970 it had 7.8 million members. The major task of the organisations and councils of VOIR is to improve the technical level of worker − rationalisers; and it defends the interests of inventors. Between 1968 and 1970, 1.5 million men studied on courses organised by them; and in 1970 there were 15,000 schools for technical training of 400,000 workers (*Partiya i rabochi klass . . .,* 1973:152). In 1965 these amateur inventors put forward 28,151,400 proposals, of which 18,537,700 were actually implemented.

For the Soviet authorities the value of such organisations is as much in providing psychological satisfaction as in economic gain. They have the effect of developing a sense of active participation in the system and attempt to make work more fulfilling for many workers. Soviet sociological studies show that not all workers participate in these activities. Lebedeva and Shkaratan (1966:241-2) have shown that it is mainly qualified workers who participate in the campaigns of invention and rationalisation: in one study they found that 90 per cent of unqualified manual workers and 37.7 per cent of qualified manual workers *never* participated; in terms of skill level, those never participating were 22 per cent of workers on the top (sixth) grade, 38 per cent on the fifth, 57 per cent on the fourth, 79 per cent on the third and 93 per cent on the first and second grades. In another survey it was found that participation in some form of social work (such as Komsomol, trade union or club activity) included 64 per cent of the workers on a 'practically always' basis, while 28 per cent 'rarely' participated and 9 per cent 'never' did. More highly skilled workers participated more often: 68 per cent of those in the fifth and sixth grades of skill participated in some form of social activity, 46 per cent of those in grades 3 and 4, and 33 per cent of workers in grades 1 and 2 (Iovchuk and Kogan, 1972a:177). While the absolute levels may indicate partly a desire by respondents to give the 'right answer', the different levels of response by various social groups give authenticity to the rankings if not to the absolute levels of response. Another study in the Urals showed that 52 per cent of workers regularly participated as members of their collective (in brigades, etc.) and another 34 per cent said that they participated 'sometimes' (Iovchuk and Kogan, 1972a:195).

Similar forms of social differentiation can be seen when attitudes towards socio-political activity are studied. Iovchuk and Kogan

TABLE 2.1 *Attitudes to socio-political activity (%)*

Attitude			*Education of respondents*			
	—4th class	*5-6 class*	*7-8 class*	*9-11 class*	*Secondary specialist*	*Complete and incomplete higher*
Favourable	77.4	79.3	88.0	86.1	87.6	96.0
Indifferent	18.7	19.2	11.8	12.8	12.4	4.0
Hostile	3.9	1.5	0.2	1.1	0	0

Source: Iovchuk and Kogan (1972a:180)

constructed Table 2.1 on the basis of an empirical study of workers' attitudes. Here we see that a relatively small proportion of the workers were hostile to socio-political activity, and of those who were, most had less than primary education. The levels of political 'indifference' fell off sharply for those who had completed more than the sixth class, and 'favourable' attitudes increased considerably. As we shall see, this is a pattern found by many studies.

Considering the number and variety of institutions that are organised in the enterprise, the general level of participation is high. White, in reviewing Soviet studies, concludes:

> By 1967, the average worker was estimated to spend an hour a week on organisational activity alone, and 45.3 per cent regarded themselves as participating in socio-political activity more generally. The average amount of time devoted to socio-political activity is estimated to have increased almost seven times over the period of Soviet rule, while the proportion of working people involved is estimated to have increased eighteen times over the same period. [White, 1975:31]

Mukhachev and Borovik's survey of 18,584 workers in twenty-one lathe-building factories found that 48 per cent of those surveyed participated actively and regularly in some organisation in the factory (Mukhachev and Borovik, 1975:21). For comparison, Kuznetsov reports a rate of 51 per cent (1974:281).

The participants were drawn (but not equally) from all strata and groups within the factories. Of the participant respondents of Mukhachev and Borovik, 38 per cent were party members, and 58 per cent were manual workers (1975:33-4). This shows important stratification of activity within the enterprise, where 14.6 per cent and 75 per cent of the workforce were party members and manual workers respectively. White summarised ten different Soviet studies of socio-political activism and has shown that the average level of participation for technical staff was 67.7 per cent (range 57.3 per cent to 84.1 per cent) and for manual workers was 35.37 per cent (20.5 – 55 per cent) (White, 1975:48).

These global figures can tell us only about levels of participation and can say nothing about the salience of that participation to the respondent. Mukhachev and Borovik attempted to measure this by asking the question: 'Do you consider it essential (*neobkhodimo*) that members of your collective take part in the administration of production?' Eleven per cent answered that it was 'completely unnecessary', 44 per cent said that they did not see the necessity for such participation by everybody, and 40.5 per cent said that such activity was 'completely necessary' (Mukhachev and Borovik, 1975:39). This latter group was formed of those who did in fact take part in the various institutions we described above.

It should be borne in mind that these data all show that many employees, especially among the manual workers, do not participate and many do not think it necessary to do so. Also, the effectiveness of much of the activity is open to question. A study of workers in the Urals questioned participants in the permanent production conferences about their effectiveness: 47 per cent thought that they improved the organisation of production, 31 per cent thought they had bettered methods of work, 30 per cent thought they strengthened production discipline, 23 per cent thought they raised the productivity of labour, 20 per cent thought they improved the quality of production and 15 per cent thought that they influenced a reduction in the cost of production (Iovchuk and Kogan, 1972a:198). Some workers who were not participants in the production conferences did not have a very high opinion of the effectiveness of many of the institutions. Complaints were made about the 'formal character' of meetings, and that the factory administration, party organs and unions often did not give sufficient attention to the organs of popular control and to proposals put to them (Iovchuk and Kogan, 1972a:204).

Disputes

We have indicated above that one of the major differences of emphasis between Western and Soviet trade unions concerns the conduct of industrial relations between management and worker. In the Soviet Union, it is assumed that the interests of management and worker are complementary rather than conflicting. In practice, however, the Soviet trade union does play a role in regulating conflict between management and worker. The union has certain responsibilities towards the settling of labour disputes. Factory trade union organisations acting with the administration set up a commission for the investigation of labour disputes, and this is the first body to which any labour dispute is referred (Smolyarchuk, 1973:153). According to McAuley, such procedures enable the great majority of disputes 'to be settled quickly at enterprise level' (McAuley, 1969:250). Official sources state that the role of the trade union in this sphere is to protect the interests of the workforce, although they also stress that trade unions must ensure that labour legislation is enforced. In practice, any issue that arises must be settled by reference to the labour code and the trade unions act thus as supportive bodies to other Soviet institutions. But this does not mean that the courts merely 'back up' the management. McAuley (1969:249) has shown that disputes between management and worker are due mainly to infringements of the law by the employers. And the union should act (though it does not always do so in practice) to enforce the law in the interests of its members. Research conducted in the 1970s in the West has shown that many grievances are referred to the courts. G. B. Smith found that about half of cases reviewed by procurial officials in the RSFSR were decided in the workers' favour (Ruble, 1977:8). Ruble's research in this respect confirms the findings of McAuley that about half of the claims for reinstatement to work were granted by the courts. 'When the courts were faced with a worker who had been dismissed without prior permission of the Factory Trade Union Committee, they usually reinstated the worker even if there had been sufficient grounds for dismissal' (Ruble, 1977:8-9).

Workers also use the union in their day-to-day exchanges with management over problems of social security benefits, bonuses, dismissal, level of wages and norms for certain jobs. Ruble has forcefully argued that since 1965 the greater proportion of bonus payable to workers has given local union officials a greater role in helping to determine workers' wages (Ruble, 1977:13). We would generally concur that at the local enterprise level the union does act positively to represent workers in their claims for 'fair' norms and grading of their occupational skill. They also have an important role to play in the allocation of housing and holiday benefits. All this makes them a political force in the industrial enterprise — though to be sure, sanctions against management in the form of strikes would not be used (see below pp. 47-9). And the most important role of the unions is in *support* of the administration's aim of increasing output. Maybe the development of Soviet unions is following a pattern not unknown in Western Europe, where the union elites are becoming intermeshed with management and government, and the locus of industrial conflict moves downward to localised shopfloor disputes. The reports in the Western press (see above p. 32) about some Soviet workers seeking means of organisation outside of the unions is an extreme manifestation of this tendency. But the situational context of the Soviet union is quite different from the West. In the USSR not only is there the formal integration of workers into the system of industrial relations, but also the Soviet worker has a very high level of job security and is most unlikely to be sacked or made redundant; in recent years too his income has steadily increased (see below, pp. 82-3).

ORGANISATIONAL STRUCTURE

The organisational structure of the Soviet factory points to some important differences in comparison with the West. The notion of a bureaucratic form of organisation derived from the work of Max Weber would not appear to be a very useful definition of the way that the factory is organised in the USSR. It is true that many of the institutions concerned with the training of the worker are 'bureaucratic' in character. Each is individually concerned with a specified number of activities; the form of organisation is hierarchical; promotion is (or should be) on merit; there are stipulated areas of competence for various officials; and organisations are achievement-orientated.

But organisational structures in the USSR would appear to us to differ in three major ways from the model drawn up by Weber. First, there is a plurality of institutional structures within any one organisation. Second, strenuous attempts are made to involve or mobilise participants in the activities of the organisation. Third, 'moral pressure' is exerted on its members. The plurality of structures is a unique characteristic of the Soviet pattern of organisations. We have seen that the director of the enterprise, the party secretary and the trade union secretary are subordinate to their various external organisations. We would like to suggest that the tendency for bureaucratic structures to be uncontrollable and to be developing along the lines of 'instrumental' or 'formal rationality' may be countered by these arrangements.

Arguing along Weberian lines, one might conclude that the ministerial representatives (the factory director) might concentrate on maximising production capabilities. However, the Party and — to a lesser extent — the trade union have a responsibility to counter these tendencies. In a Weberian sense, the Party especially has the duty to assert or to re-establish 'substantive rationality'. That is, its task is to see that the industrialist's or the professional's goals are congruent with the 'general goals' of society. The various 'rationalisation' campaigns attempt to synthesise both formal and instrumental rationality. The idea of 'control' is significant in this context. Rather than 'control' being the expression of one group's interest, it should be considered in terms of general political or economic goals that are considered to derive from the laws of development (*zakonomernosti*) of society. Put in a Weberian sense, institutions should be directed to work towards substantive rationality. In practice, however, we doubt whether the Party does have this superior role, and it seems likely that it often becomes much more a tool of management, closely identified with the fulfilment of the factory's economic plans (Lane, 1978:chapter 10). There is a tension between theory and practice.

The other major way in which Soviet organisational structures differ from those in the West is that they require a greater degree of formal commitment or participation. Such participation is within the hierarchical structure we have described and it does not diminish the responsibility of the management. Rather, the large number of formal groups seek to involve the worker in various forms of activity. This is an attempt to solve the problem of motivational commitment resulting from large-scale organisation of workers having few means of expression. While we are unable to prove this scientifically because no systematic comparative research has been done, general levels of participation, even taking into account bias in Soviet reporting, appear to be higher than in the West.

CHAPTER 3

The 'Alienated' or
the 'Incorporated' Worker?

It is difficult to ascertain with accuracy how the institutional setting influences the social attitudes, the psychological state or level of alienation of the industrial worker. The Soviet industrial worker creates a world of objects. For Marxists such 'objectification' does not necessarily lead to 'alienation'. Alienation takes place only under certain social conditions, when man's product assumes an existence not only external to man but also alien to him: 'Man's labour becomes an object, an external existence, . . . something alien to him and becomes a power on its own confronting him' (K. Marx, 'Economic and Philosophical Manuscripts', in Burns, 1969:97). Man's product is exploited from him; in terms of commodities it is sold and creates capital. Capital in the shape of machinery owned by a ruling class threatens man's existence, through the creation of unemployment, and through making possible an increasing division of labour — though the division of labour and the existence of capital are not in themselves alienative.

Manifestations of this basic alienation are seen in the attitudes of men towards work, towards other men and towards society. Labour is no longer a creative activity developing man's potential, but becomes an instrumental activity. 'Man does not affirm himself in his work, but denies himself . . . he does not develop freely his physical and mental energy but mortifies his body and ruins his mind' (Burns, 1969:99). Relations between men assume an 'alienative' form; man becomes estranged from other men. This again, in Marx's view, is caused by ownership relations: the worker's product is ,/alienated from him; it has been appropriated by 'some other man than the worker', the capitalist, 'in the service, under the domination, the coercion and the yoke' of whom the worker is forced to produce (Burns, 1969:105). Marx thus sees the source of alienation in capitalist property relations and not in technological factors: the division of

40

labour and the growth of capital-intensive industries lead to alienation only under conditions of the separation of ownership from the working class.

Many contemporary Western studies of alienation analyse components of workers' attitudes independently of ownership relations. Blauner (1964), for instance, in his work on American workers, identifies four components of alienation: powerlessness, meaninglessness, social isolation and self-estrangement. This is, to be charitable, a reinterpretation of Marx, for Blauner considers the essence of alienation, or rather of attitudes towards and happiness in work, to be derived from technological factors, not property relations. This is not the same as the essentially structural conditioning of alienation meant by Marx. It is important not to confuse these two kinds of relationships. We shall argue here that alienation in a Marxist structural sense is not directly applicable to the Soviet worker's situation. But 'alienation', in the sense of dissatisfaction with work, with instrumental attitudes, with forms of 'powerlessness' over the work situation, is still a feature of the Soviet worker and in some ways is comparable to Western non-Marxist studies of workers' attitudes. Alienation then may be said to have a multi-dimensional character: psychological, social, economic and political, deriving from non-property factors. Ownership of the means of production is not in the hands of a *class,* analogous to a ruling capitalist class; but, as the USSR is a transitional society, the working class does not directly control property. The state rules on behalf of the working class rather than there being direct working-class decision-making — albeit incorporating many forms of participation and mobilisation of the industrial worker. To this extent we disagree with Shkaratan, cited above (p. 3), that the Soviet working class is a class 'for itself'. Control of the means of production is essentially centralised, but mediated by various forms of checking (*kontrol'*) by various groups of workers at the industrial enterprise. We would also disagree with Ticktin's analysis that 'the [political?] elite have only limited control over the surplus [of labour] — more limited than under capitalism' (Ticktin, 1976:43). Rather we see a more effectively socialised and incorporated working class: groups of workers may influence and even seek to change the pattern of exchange between themselves and the political elite, but the working class has little independent class power to resist government action. Much more important are differences of interest and attitudes between various strata of workers within the enterprise; such interests should be seen as stemming from their place in the division of labour; and, as we shall see, some workers are more effectively 'incorporated' than others.

Data collected by Zdravomyslov and Yadov (1966) help to show the extent of dissatisfaction of workers with their work. The authors interviewed 2665 young Leningrad workers and constructed an index measuring 'satisfaction with occupation'. Again we would be cautious about interpreting the results and would focus on the different responses of various groups, rather than on absolute levels of satisfaction. The authors found that satisfaction with occupation varied from a negative attitude among unskilled manual labour to a highly positive one among the highly skilled. The 'social significance of work' is another measure of worker attitude, and here we again find that the more highly qualified workers (especially panel-setters) had positive attitudes, while the unskilled manual workers did not, and the machine operators also had a low score (Zdravomyslov and Yadov, 1966:108). The factors in the work situation that gave rise to satisfaction were: content of work (index score 0.72), pay (0.61), possibility of improving skill (0.58), variety in work (0.48), organisation of labour (0.38), management's concern for workers (0.35), physical effort (0.32) (Zdravomyslov and Yadov, 1966:114). Pay came relatively high in the list and certain groups of workers regarded it more highly than others.

A study of motorcar workers in Gor'ki (1965-73) found that 26.3 per cent of a sample of workers estimated high wages to be the most important aspect of work, 32.4 per cent thought 'love of their trade' most important, and 39.6 per cent put in first place 'solidarity and friendship in the collective'. Consideration of workers with bad discipline records (about 9 per cent of the workforce) found a different distribution: high wages was given most importance by 52 per cent of these workers, love of a trade by 23 per cent and solidarity with the collective by 14.5 per cent (Podorov, 1976:74). Another study reported by Shkaratan showed that participation in voluntary social activity varied by occupational group of workers. Those with the greatest level of participation were management (84 per cent), qualified non-manuals (82.4 per cent) and highly qualified manuals (tool-setters) (79.2 per cent); at the very bottom come unqualified manual workers (35.1 per cent), office workers (54.5 per cent) and machine operators (54.3 per cent) (Shkaratan, 1967:36).

These data are not dissimilar to those revealed by studies

conducted in the West. Greater dissatisfaction exists among unskilled workers doing repetitive jobs than among more skilled workers; manual workers have no control over the rhythm of their work. The perception of the social significance of work is lowest among the unskilled manual groups. Pay is important and is regarded in many ways as instrumental: work is not an end in itself, but a means to an end. Money does not, however, have the salience it has for Lockwood's 'privatised' worker. He writes as follows: 'The single, overwhelmingly important, and most spontaneously conceived criterion of class division is money, and the possessions, both material and immaterial, that money can buy' (Lockwood, 1966, in Bulmer, 1975:24). While money is relatively more important for certain strata of Soviet workers than others, it does not command the same power as for the 'privatised' worker because in the USSR money does not have the same salience in terms of possessions (both as investment and income) that it commands under capitalism.

I disagree

Other studies have come to conclusions similar to those of Shkaratan and Yadov. Aitov's interviews with 10,707 workers in Ufa in 1972 showed that attitude towards work was most positive among the more qualified and educated workers. Dividing the workforce into four groups by level of complexity of work, it was found that, the higher the group in terms of work complexity, the greater was the satisfaction with work: in Group 1, 61.6 per cent of the respondents said that 'work' was the 'part of [their] activity which gives most satisfaction'; for Group 2 ('qualified workers') the figure was 43 per cent, for Group 3 ('lowly qualified') it was 44.7 per cent and for Group 4 ('unqualified') it fell to 37.4 per cent (Aitov, 1974:63). Similar grading of rates of participation occurred for party membership: Group 1 — 13.1 per cent; Group 2 — 7.7 per cent; Group 3 — 5.0 per cent; Group 4 — 3.1 per cent. Similarly, for membership of the movement for rationalisers and inventors: Group 1 — 16.2 per cent; Group 2 — 17.9 per cent; Group 3 — 8.3 per cent and Group 4 — 6.1 per cent (Aitov, 1974:63).

These studies, if we concentrate on the rankings, confirm the stratification of the Soviet industrial working class by occupation, level of skill and education that we observed above. Mukhachev and Borovik again found variations in the attitudes of different groups of workers when they tried to study general 'ownership relations' towards the factory. They asked the question (in sixteen lathe-building factories), 'Do you consider yourself to be one of the proprietors [*khozyaev*] of socialist production?' 47.2 per cent said yes; 22.5 per cent, no; 22.1 per cent did not know and 8.2 per cent did not answer (Mukhachev and Borovik, 1975:53-4). Those who actually participated in the various institutions of control of the production process had the more positive attitudes towards socialist property. By implication, workers with higher levels of education and occupational position would appear to have higher levels of 'consciousness'.

It cannot be denied that many workers are dissatisfied with work. Such dissatisfaction, in our view, is determined partly by the technology of modern industry, which — in both the USSR and the West — requires many workers to be involved in routine production. Many of these workers see factory labour as instrumental. A secondary factor giving rise to job dissatisfaction is the incapacity of the system to provide a sufficient number of jobs requiring the levels of education and attainment achieved by workers. Third, there are imperfect and contradictory forms of socialisation: these in practice tend to emphasise achievement through qualifications at the expense of minimising the desirability of manual unskilled work. There is then among Soviet industrial workers a certain lack of unity between man and his work, between subject and object. Whether this amounts to 'alienation' in a *Marxist* sense is debatable, and we would say that these attitudes rather are evidence of work dissatisfaction. The Soviet worker is still subject to various forms of estrangement from his work, his fellow men and his environment; and some groups of workers may even form an alienative sub-culture. It is particularly important to note that the worker does not directly control the means of production. But we would disagree with writers such as Blumberg who argue that the relation to the means of production by Soviet workers is the same as under capitalism. 'State management of the economy perpetuates the alienation of the worker from the means of production, for he has no more control over them than he ever did' (Blumberg, 1968:177). 'Control' is only one element of alienation, and we would suggest that the relationship to the means of production has undergone a structural change; this places all employees, management and workers in a factory in essentially the same class relations to the means of production, which is not the case under capitalism. Soviet industrialisation has involved the allocation of use-values for investment as well as for consumer goods and not, as some commentators erroneously believe, the production of exchange values for profit. (See the useful discussion in Therborn,

1976:382.) The extraction of surplus is utilised not for the direct benefit of a managerial ruling class, but mainly for investment in society as a whole — even though it might be conceded that in particular cases forms of 'unequal exchange' favour the managerial groups. This makes for a greater homogeneity of *class* interest (in a narrow Marxist sense) of managers and workers and of the various interests making up the Soviet factory. What is true, however, is that there is a stratification among the workforce. Though there are exceptions, the more highly skilled and educated groups among the workforce have greater positive commitment to the work process and to 'control' within the framework of Soviet management. What is absent, as many critics of Soviet society have noted, is direct management by the working class, and this gives rise even in a Marxist sense to partial forms of alienation. It should be emphasised that, because class relations are common, this does not imply that there is a unity of interest between the various groups working in the Soviet enterprise; there are important social distinctions stemming from the social and cultural division of labour, occupation being the most salient.

THE 'INCORPORATED' WORKER

On the admittedly inadequate and somewhat fragmentary data at our disposal, it is impossible to make a definitive statement about the work orientations and socio-political attitudes of the Soviet working class in general. Indeed, one of our conclusions is that the working class is *socially* stratified, rather than homogeneous. Lockwood (1966, reprinted in Bulmer, 1975) and others have attempted to categorise three main types of working-class milieux: the traditional, the deferential and the privatised. To this we would add a fourth ideal type, which we believe is more apposite to the Soviet worker: the incorporated. We would stress here the fact that by an 'ideal type' we do not imply any ethical values; nor do we wish to suggest that we include all aspects of the life of all industrial workers in the USSR. What we are attempting is to provide a construct that provides a limiting case, as it were, and that we hope may constitute a basis for generalisation and comparison. We do this in the belief that the Soviet industrial worker both differs from and has certain similarities to his Western counterpart.

The traditional 'proletarian' worker under conditions of modern capitalism is part of a highly homogeneous social group with respect to life-styles. Also he sees society in essentially dichotomous power terms: of 'them' and 'us' (Lockwood, 1966, in Bulmer, 1975:18). Alec Nove to some extent has attempted a similar power type of analysis of Soviet society: he makes a 'qualitative distinction between . . . "we" and "they", between rulers and ruled . . .'. Nove asserts that this imagery of society 'impregnates people's consciousness in the Soviet Union' (Nove, 1975:624). No evidence at all is marshalled to support this contention, and we feel that the centre of gravity is misplaced in this model. We would agree that there appear to be closely knit social networks among factory workers that 'emphasise mutual aid in everyday life and the obligation to join in the gregarious pattern of leisure which may express itself in a public and present-oriented conviviality . . .' (Lockwood, 1966, in Bulmer, 1975:17). Also, party organisations are located here — unlike under capitalism. The worker's identification with his productive enterprise is strengthened at all points by the structural arrangements of Soviet society. But we have found no evidence to suggest that the Soviet working class as such has developed an alternative counter-culture to the values of the dominant one of Marxism-Leninism. (On sub-cultural differences see Ol'shanski, 1965:503 *et seq.*) By this we mean that there are no articulated sets of values that reject and seek to replace those defined by the elites. Study of deviance in the USSR has yet to uncover any institutional opposition by the working class (see Tökés, 1975). Rather, these traditional life-styles are fostered by the factory. One radical critic of Soviet power sees 'working class opposition [being] expressed principally through so called "deviance" and "social problems" ' (Holubenko, 1975:8). Holubenko points out that drunkenness is the 'most prevalent outlet for frustration' (1975:8). But drunkenness, however important, is not an exclusive expression of the Soviet working class, and is as much a Russian cultural and peasant artefact as a working-class one (Connor, 1972:39); some studies suggest that the incidence of drunkenness among the working class is greatest among the less well-educated and less well-skilled strata (Tundykov, 1967:47). The phenomenon is more likely to be explained in terms of traditional Russian culture, the strains of industrialisation, and maladjustment to urban life and to factory work, than as an expression of political discontent. Such 'traditional' attitudes do not appear to be linked to protest in the form of strikes.

Our knowledge about strikes is extremely fragmentary and unreliable. Holubenko points out that they take place in 'areas removed from the Moscow—Leningrad region', in the 'periphery' of the country (1975:8). This again would suggest (as far as our interest here is concerned) that such activity is linked to the newly mobilised working class, rather than being an expression of traditional solidarity. Unlike Habermas, who has analysed traditions in the West in terms of supports and buttresses to the dominant culture of capitalism, we see traditionalism at the place of work in the USSR as undermining the system of industrial production. This is because in Russian culture before the revolution there had hardly developed a work ethic comparable to the Western 'Protestant ethic', which underpinned capitalist development (see Habermas, 1976:77).

The 'deferential' worker views his bosses with respect; he perceives himself in a legitimately inferior position; he provides his labour in return for the traditional expertise and paternalism of the management. Our study would suggest again that this stratified yet complementary world of management and worker is untrue of the Soviet Union. The Soviet worker does not regard his leaders as having 'the intrinsic qualities of an ascriptive elite' (Lockwood, 1966, in Bulmer, 1975:18), though they may be regarded as pursuing the 'national interest'. The levels of participation in management and politics by the Soviet worker, and his higher levels of aspiration and mobility, lead us to conclude that deferentiality is not a major trait of Soviet workers. What does seem to be a feature of the structure of Soviet industrial workers is that they are brought 'into direct association with [their] employers or other middle class influentials and hinder[ed] from forming strong attachments to workers in a similar market situation to [their] own' (Lockwood, 1966, in Bulmer, 1975:19). This would suggest that there is an integration of worker and management — but not of the traditionalist deferential type.

The 'privatised' worker is one who is isolated at work and in the community: social divisions are seen in terms of 'differences in income and material possessions' (Lockwood, 1966, in Bulmer, 1975:21). His work is instrumental; the money nexus predominates. Such workers may be in trade unions, but union membership is not the 'symbolic expression of an affective attachment to a working class community but a utilitarian association for achieving his private goal of a rising standard of living' (Lockwood, 1966, in Bulmer, 1975:23). The latter could not be said of union membership in the

USSR. The privatised worker is apathetic; he does not question the political, economic and social arrangements that confront him. In the USSR some of the orientations of a privatised worker in our view may be shared by a member of a sub-culture: i.e. a group that does not subscribe to all the major values of a society and that has different priorities from the governing elites. Podorov's investigation of violators of labour discipline found not only that this group of men (only 8 per cent were women) was interested in work mainly for instrumental pecuniary reasons, but also that their interests were mainly passive, revolving around drinking, meeting friends and playing dominoes; they rarely participated (1 per cent) in social activity, or read educative literature (Podorov, 1976:73-4). But such pecuniary interests are not part of a 'privatised' worker's world as stipulated in Lockwood's model. As Lockwood points out, a pecuniary model of society can be internalised by a worker only in so far as 'his social environment supports such an interpretation' (Lockwood, 1966, in Bulmer, 1975:26). Despite a movement towards a consumer revolution in the USSR, no Soviet theory (or counter-ideology) supports such an interpretation.

Workers who are 'privatised' are apolitical, but it would be incorrect to view such men as in principle being not prone to strike activity. On the contrary, in theory workers' expectations for a higher standard of living may be so strongly internalised that if they are not met — through increases in wages — then intense industrial conflict may occur. Such conflict is essentially economistic and does not entail any criticism of the political order. The strikes that occurred in Novocherkassk in 1962 (Boiter, 1964) were in protest against price rises and increased work norms, as were other cases of trouble in 1963 (Brown, 1966:235). Much of Holubenko's analysis may be interpreted in this vein. He emphasises the fact that industrial unrest has occurred 'in response to three basic issues: (a) low wages — in particular a sudden drop in bonuses or in wages due to revised work norms announced by the factory management; (b) food and consumer goods shortages; (c) inadequate housing' (Holubenko, 1975:14). We must emphasise along with Brown (1966) and McAuley (1969) that strikes in the Soviet Union are exceptional events: not only are they mediated by labour disputes procedures and other methods of control, but the Soviet worker 'lacks any tradition of pressing for improvements' (McAuley, 1969:251). While Holubenko concedes that strikes in the Soviet Union are 'localised events' that raise 'limited demands' (1975:16), owing to the fragmented character of the working class, he sees the development of a hereditary proletariat as leading to class-consciousness. We see no evidence of this tendency in the sense of a political counter-culture or, as writers such as Westergaard would define it, a 'radical class consciousness' involving a 'recognition of common interests of wage workers in other occupations' and a 'tentative vision of an "alternative society"' (Westergaard, 1975:251-2). Ticktin also emphasises the present 'atomisation' of the Soviet working class (1976:39-40). (Ticktin, though, apart from this point, could not be considered to support the views of this school.)

We would agree, however, that socialisation is not completely successful. Sub-cultures persist whose values are incongruous with those of the political elites. Absenteeism and drunkenness appear to be the major 'counter-values'. Such values are not distributed randomly among the population: men who are less well educated and those in unskilled manual jobs are more prone to adopt these life-styles. They are derived, in our view, from traditional peasant-type orientations exacerbated by the inadequate conditions of Soviet urban life. But overall we would agree with Bronfenbrenner's view that political education (in its broadest sense) is effective since the norms of schoolchildren and the norms of adults are similar (cited in Cary, 1974:458). We would not expect such 'deviant' attitudes to have any significant political implications. More important, we believe, are the conflicting goals that are part of the socialisation process (see below, chapter 4) and also the relatively lower exposure of many of the 'violators of discipline' to the socialisation process.

Soviet management—worker relations pay a great deal of attention to the need for material incentives, which in our view are likely to increase as the economy matures for, as both Soviet sociologists and Holubenko have pointed out, economistic considerations play an important role in worker motivation. But the cash nexus is not yet as dominating as it is under Western capitalism. The data we have considered also lead us to reject the view that the working class as such may be typified by sentiments of apathy, or that its social role is one of isolation. Rather the opposite: participation and stratification seem to us to be more important.

Whatever its limitations, the typology of the 'privatised worker' does provide us with an explanation of the basis of social solidarity for the modern industrial worker. If a man does not work for the monetary return he gets from his labour, then why should he work under the conditions of modern capitalistic industry? Many critics of the Soviet Union ranging from Conquest to Holubenko have emphasised the role of coercion and repression. We would change the emphasis considerably to take into account socialisation and incorporation of the working class. The 'incorporated worker' shares many of the traits we have found in the above ideal types: he has certain forms of solidarity with the factory; he accepts the authority structure on the basis of its performance capacity; he participates actively in improving production; and he is closer to the administration both socially and politically than the worker in capitalist society. But he does not actively shape the overriding values of his society, which are determined largely by the ruling political elites. While there are tendencies towards 'privatisation' of life in the sense that family orientation (not discussed in this book) and economistic attitudes are strengthening, the dominant ideology of Marxism—Leninism and the institutional forms of polity and economy place these attitudes in a quite different context from the 'privatised' worker in the West. We see such 'privatisation' leading to an *apolitical* status rather than, as suggested by Habermas, a growing politicisation of private life: this is because, following the October Revolution, the family, at least in urban areas, was weakened in its traditional 'solidaristic' functions. These indeed are currently being strengthened in the Soviet Union and the family is becoming a more important form of integration. Also, the worker is not only used to a steadily rising standard of living and social benefits, but he is also guaranteed permanency in employment.

Westergaard (1975:255-6) has called for attention to be directed to the 'macro-structural' features of societies that promote or hinder class identity and opposition. The structural features of Soviet society undoubtedly severely inhibit opposition. The incorporation of the worker is ensured by the pervading but not perfect forms of socialisation and by the interlocking institutional arrangements of Soviet society and factory. What the Soviet political and administrative system has succeeded in doing is to provide mechanisms to integrate a relatively unsophisticated labour force into the industrial system. The dynamics of the system lead to the incorporation of the natural leaders among the workers — not only by occupational promotion, but also through the Party and other organisations, the worker becomes increasingly identified with the factory. The Soviet working class is non-revolutionary and has some attitudes in common with the British working class. It is inculcated with pragmatic aspirations, and a general conception of serving the 'national interest' (see McKenzie and Silver, 1968). But the Soviet worker is part of an egalitarian and contest educational system (discussed further below, pp. 92-3), where he can progress if he succeeds in open competition occurring throughout his school career (rather than a more sponsored system as in Britain): as a result of the opportunities open to him he has high levels of occupational aspiration. This is 'cooled out' through an endless process of educational selection. As Brown has emphasised in an earlier study, there are many channels open to a worker to resolve disputes (Brown, 1966:236-8). The worker finds his immediate demands fulfilled at least to some extent by his employers and by the ruling elites (but Ticktin overplays, to our mind, the accommodating nature of the authorities). Here stability of employment and a rising living standard are important. The major problem facing the system is whether pragmatic economistic expectations may be met in future by the political and economic system providing a rising standard of living. If the system does not, our prognosis would be that disillusionment would lead to discontent, which would be contained within the system. Essentially, this is because socialisation is relatively efficient and prevents the aggregation of a radical alternative, and because the institutional, ideological and social structures are conducive to the formation of an incorporated working class. At most what is possible is that groups of workers may seek to change the priorities between them and other groups. The relative strength of various groups of workers at the enterprise may be reflected in changing wage differentials. In terms of wage payments, the tendency has been for the manual working strata to improve their position *vis à vis* ITRs (see below pp. 82-3).

The industrial worker is to a large degree moulded by the system in which he finds himself. While there are processes of exchange between the worker and the elites, these are dominated by the values and the institutions of the political elites. Our picture is of a worker fairly well incorporated into the institutions. We disagree with writers such as, on the one hand, Ticktin who see a form of paralysis in the structural arrangements with the workers being able to exert considerable autonomous power over the political bureaucracy, and, on the other, Conquest, who see workers having absolutely no influence. The greater active incorporation of the worker under state socialism will be understood by study of the process by which the Soviet worker is socialised. It is remarkable that studies of the orientations of Soviet workers in the West have not examined in any detail the ways in which attitudes are transmitted. In our view, the educational system is the leading institution of the ideological apparatus. It shapes the worker's attitude to work and largely determines the kind of work he will do; it also has an important role in political socialisation. We shall turn therefore to a discussion of the ways in which the elites define the 'right attitude' towards work. In later chapters we shall see how in practice labour discipline, job choice and material rewards operate.

CHAPTER 4

Defining the 'Right Attitudes' Towards Work

How a society selects, classifies, distributes and evaluates the educational knowledge it considers to be public, reflects both the distribution of power and the principles of social control. [Bernstein, 1971:184]

Trade training and labour education are important in all industrial societies, but in the Soviet Union they have played a special and significant role. Policies of rapid economic growth required as a corollary the training of skilled workers, technicians and engineers to man the factories. The economic returns from education have . been a big stimulus to the development of, and investment in, education in the USSR. Labour education has to be seen also in the context of Soviet ideology — in the peculiar way that Marxist-Leninist ideas have evolved to form a pattern of thought about the ways man *ought* to be educated and trained in a socialist society. Labour education is concerned not only with technical skills but with inculcating general attitudes — to work, to one's fellow men and to society as a whole. In this aspect of education, the inculcation of values and norms is crucial to the transmission of knowledge. The educational system must mediate the demands of the economy and of the political system, and the patterns of occupational and status differentiation. The flow of recruits to and from the educational system is influenced by the decisions of government and also by less tangible but no less impartial sentiments about the status of occupational roles. In Soviet industrial society, levels of educational competence and attainment become central to placement in the system of stratification.

These various demands on the educational system give it somewhat conflicting roles to perform. From the ideological point of view, instruction should be egalitarian, providing equal facilities for all students with the aim of educating all to a common level. But to operate efficiently in an economic sense, selection must be made between students with unequal ability and motivation. A process of selection occurs by which students of varying abilities are sorted out into different educational categories in which they are subject to both general socialisation and training in specific skills. In the vocational sphere these two tasks are closely related, for skills are performed in the context of work, and attitudes to work and to authority are important components of the application of industrial skills. But allocation to institutions performing specialised roles comes into conflict with egalitarian ideology — for educational institutions differentiate between their pupils in terms of the level of knowledge they impart and thereby determine the placement of the student in the labour market.

Placement in the occupational structure involves allocation to a place in the system of social stratification. In this process of selection and placement numerous problems may arise. The educational system must as best it can match up the ambitions of the student on the one hand with his ability and on the other with the available jobs. In the USSR, the occupational expectations of the population involve the development of ambition on a scale that we shall show cannot be met by the number and distribution of jobs available in the economy. The control of ambition is something that the educational system may attempt, but in this effort it is dependent on the wider system of values. Educational institutions then must try to reconcile the pattern of student ambition (the demand for jobs) and the attainment of status position through placement in the occupational hierarchy (given the supply of jobs available).

In addition to placement, the educational system also performs the important role of socialisation. Socialisation may be defined as the process by which the values and norms of a society are transmitted from one generation to another. Educational institutions allow the political elites, who may control the content and the process of education, to interpose values different from those held by the family or peer group. In this way the school system may be used by the political elites as an instrument of social change and political mobilisation.

The values and beliefs that are transmitted in educational systems are of three different kinds: those concerning interpersonal social relations in general, those inculcating attitudes to work and leisure and involving an attitude towards time, and those that legitimate the existing structure and process of the political system. A high degree of congruence may prevail between the values of the established political elites and other sources of values such as the mass media or family. If there is a high level of integration, the 'community of assumptions' (Etzioni, 1968:117) shared by members of a society may be maintained by the schools without conscious effort. This is a most effective way of socialising attitudes, for the process appears effortless and pupils come to 'take for granted' particular assumptions and processes. In societies where there is incongruence and a lack of integration between mass and elite values, then the school system is used overtly to inculcate values that are explicit rather than implicit in the curriculum. A society that is undergoing various kinds of modernisation or revolutionary change is characterised by educational systems (and other media) being explicit in propagandising the values of the ruling class. In the Soviet Union, against the backdrop of a traditional peasant society, the schools have been agents that have attempted to inculcate attitudes of loyalty to the communist régime, to the ideals of Marxism-Leninism and to the practices of the ruling Communist Party. These processes we define as political socialisation. Other aspects of socialisation are more general: for the industrial worker they involve the creation of positive attitudes towards work, the acceptance of authority, general striving and a mastery of the environment.

In the legitimating ideology, the industrial worker has an important place; for the communist state rules on behalf of the working class, and, as we saw above, the industrial worker in Marxist theory (being a producer of value) is a crucial element in the structure of the working class. In practice, however, the 'officially sponsored' values are not always logically consistent with each other, and in the sphere of the education of industrial workers there are important conflicts over priorities.

In this chapter we shall examine the methods of socialisation and the values that the elites seek to inculcate. We have appended a section on institutional control to illustrate how these values are put into effect in the technical trade school (see Appendix A). Chapter 5 will be specifically concerned with the effectiveness of the process of control of the worker and of inculcating the work values desired. Finally, in chapters 6 and 7 we turn to discuss the demand for kinds of educational institutions and occupations when we consider the level of ambition and attainment of Soviet school-leavers.

Work Values and Norms

In the USSR the educational system is explicitly and systematically used as a major instrument of socialisation and many people and organisations have prescribed roles to play in the process of forming the character of workers of the future.

The four overriding orientations to labour that the elites seek to inculcate may be summarised under the following major headings:

(1) 'Discipline is necessary for efficient work';
(2) 'Work is a basic fulfilment of one's life';
(3) 'All jobs are worthy of respect'; and
(4) 'The better one works and the more one studies, the more one contributes to the Motherland'.

Let us consider each of these in turn.

Discipline is necessary for efficient work

The first of these requirements, discipline, is considered to be necessary in all spheres of Soviet life. Soviet society is directed towards the attainment of 'the glorious future under Communism' at the expense of a comfortable present, and discipline has the effect of helping Soviet citizens to accept a frequently harsh today for the sake of a better tomorrow. The Soviet authorities are also eager to instil a deep sense of discipline in their citizens, since it helps the operation of a modernising political party anxious to influence almost every aspect of the life of a large modern state. Just as discipline aids efficient control by a small leadership in any wartime country, so it facilitates party control in the Soviet Union where an atmosphere of warlike struggle is sometimes created to stimulate the population to unified endeavour. At the place of work, in all modern industrial societies, there is an attempt to achieve maximum production through a disciplined, obedient and responsive workforce.

An important aspect of labour discipline, especially in the Soviet situation with its stress on collectivist behaviour, is the ability to work efficiently and harmoniously in teams. A pattern of work organised in teams is extensively seen throughout the USSR. In many schools pupils are organised into brigades following the pattern of their parents' factory brigades. In each brigade there are three or four pupils who choose one of their number as brigadier. From the whole class (comprising four to six brigades) a senior brigadier is elected. It is claimed that 'such organisation provides the necessary conditions for a collective—independent unit — leadership and subordination, mutual interest in work and a common goal' (Liferov and Dobrusin, 1969:69). It must be noted that the Soviet concept of the collective always implies a group with a leader, rather than a group all of whose members have equivalent functions. In the pupils' collectives all are trained in the habit of accepting the authority of one leader (whose powers are often legitimated by the fact that he has been elected by the group as a whole). Brigade-leaders, however, have at least as many duties as powers. (For details see Liferov and Dobrusin, 1969:68.) Most children will, of course, take their turn at being a brigade-leader during their school career and so all will experience the training in discipline and responsibility that these duties provide.

With its emphasis on disciplined behaviour in a collectivist environment, the labour training lesson at the Soviet general school sets up a microcosm of Soviet society (training pupils to accept and fit into the system outside the classroom as well). Moreover, authority is emphasised as bringing many responsibilities to those who in any measure hold it and citizens are taught to regard participation in terms of duties as well as of rights.

The lessons in discipline learnt at the general school are reinforced by what the pupil is later taught at the vocational school or when he starts work at a factory. One very common method used to encourage a positive attitude towards work is the system of 'socialist emulation', and this acts as a compulsive form of discipline. Honour (and disgrace) in these emulation processes are ultimately given legitimacy in terms of the collective rather than of the individual.

Vocational (or technical trade) schools' notice-boards display photographs of pupils who have distinguished their group, their class or their institution by shining in some type of competition. Reproach for poor performance is similarly publicly expressed. A Dagestan glass factory, for example, has its own satirical newspaper which 'does all it can to create a low level of tolerance towards perpetuators of relics of the past' (Il'yasov, 1971:48). 'Relics of the past' may refer to unsatisfactory behaviour, productivity, attendance, discipline or social activity. Since late 1975, and reinforced by the directives of the twenty-fifth Party Congress (in 1976), competitions have emphasised quality and efficiency, rather than mere quantity of output. It must not be assumed that industrial competitions limit themselves to indices of productivity. They can be related to general matters of social concern — with work discipline or workers' use of leisure time (whether they devote themselves to study and voluntary social work in, say, the Party or the trade union). Once again, the praises or reproaches given for success or failure in the competitions are expressed in collectivist terms, and they act powerfully to discipline the individual and to bind him or her to the collective.

Work is a basic fulfilment of one's life

The second tenet fundamental to socialisation in Soviet labour education is that 'work is a basic fulfilment of one's life'; this is even more cardinal to Soviet morality in general. In Soviet society the ultimate goal is to achieve communism. The way in which the individual is encouraged to give his life meaning is by working as hard as he can towards the attainment of communism on Soviet soil — and it is through his everyday labour, in industry or on the land, that he is shown to be contributing most towards the future perfection of society. Work has a very important role to play in the Soviet moral code, for it provides the ordinary person's life with some kind of transcendent significance. On a more practical level it is obviously advantageous to the authorities to promote a work ethic because, just as with Weber's Protestant ethic, such a value system encourages productive effort and legitimates abstinence and investment. In this way work is treated as the basic fulfilment of man's life in Soviet society in order both to promote productivity and to provide purpose to life for the Soviet citizen.

This goal is summed up by two Soviet educationalists, who state:

> The most important task of character education of the new man is to educate young people with the habit and the need to work conscientiously according to their abilities for the general good and to see in this the main purpose of life, its joy and its happiness. [Ivanovich and Epshteyn, 1972:33]

They suggest that the following methods are particularly useful to foster such an attitude in schoolchildren: work in teams; use of 'socialist competition'; and use of the 'heroic examples' of leaders and innovators in production work (Ivanovich and Epshteyn,

1968:36). The first two of these methods serve to make work more enjoyable by turning it into something more social and (in the second) into a kind of game. The third approach is the commonly used one of providing children with heroes to emulate, and here these are not football-players or pop-stars as in the West, but the more everyday heroes of labour. These three methods in slightly different ways all help to put across the concept of work as fulfilment and as a pleasure to the Soviet citizen. Although Ivanovich and Epshteyn mention the methods in relation to schoolchildren, they are also used on the shop floor. Perhaps the most common way in which the principle of work as fulfilment is fostered is through the frequent display of the slogan *Slava trudu* (Glory to labour), which appears on the fronts of buses and on illuminated signs or banners on public buildings. Soviet values are work-oriented and production-linked rather than designed to extol today's satisfaction or immediate gratification. They do not provide the kind of consumer ethic that is linked to the pecuniary strivings of the privatised worker discussed above (chapter 3).

Are all jobs equally worthy of respect?

As the third and fourth principles of labour socialisation are really opposite sides of the same coin, it is convenient to discuss these two principles together. The third element — 'all jobs are worthy of respect' — has a significant part to play in Soviet morality, for it is one of the Soviet values that can be said to follow from Marx's teaching. (The much-promoted Soviet sentiment of patriotism, on the other hand, was condemned by both Marx and Lenin.) Though Marx recognised the division between manual and non-manual labour that existed under capitalism, he emphasised the interdependence of all types of labour and the important role of manual labour as a source of wealth. This motif, by emphasising that all jobs are equal under socialism, in contrast to the situation under capitalism where there are exploited and exploiters, seeks to substantiate the claim of equality in a society that in many respects is manifestly unequal. It may also be significant for the personal peace of mind of those Soviet citizens who have to accept humble jobs, for it provides an alternative form of respect from achievement and technical competence.

It must not be assumed from this that Soviet morality puts a low value on achievement. Under the fourth precept listed above we subsume two motifs ('the better one works' and 'the more one studies, the more one contributes to the Motherland') that seem to contradict the preceding egalitarian principle as they emphasise the unequal social and economic effects of study and labour. Since the time of Stalin's ascendancy, wage levels have been determined by the levels of skill and by the performance of a task. Skill level is defined in terms of complexity and difficulty of a task and is thus directly linked to the educational qualifications and experience of the worker. These values are in contradiction to the third principle, for the implication is that manual unqualified labour is less valuable than work requiring more skill or training. This principle is promulgated by the Soviet authorities because it helps to stimulate ambition, and legitimates the reward of certain kinds of work. As the industrialisation process requires many skilled and technically qualified men and women, the authorities have been anxious to foster a reverence for study and for highly skilled labour. By encouraging all to compete for the highest levels of training, it is hoped that the most talented people, regardless of social background, will win through to the top ranks of the system. It has been taken to an extreme point by the suggestion that one day everyone will have a higher education, thereby enabling the best to be chosen for the most difficult jobs (*Komsomol'skaya pravda*, 16 March 1973, *CDSP*, vol. 25, no. 30, pp. 31-2).

It has been seen that the notion, 'all jobs are worthy of respect', conflicts to some degree with the principle, 'the more one studies and works, the more one contributes to the Motherland'. Occasionally conflict situations result from the clash of these two principles, and when this happens it seems to us that it is the latter that has usually triumphed. The pragmatic achievement-oriented value, which is a spur to productivity, has been promoted at the expense of the principle that asserts the equality of labour. There are no tangible prizes given for the fulfilment of egalitarian norms.

If we consider specifically the egalitarian motif, we find that it has been fostered largely by such means as the telling of stories about labouring men, presenting them not as ordinary but as heroes, and by showing history to have been created not so much by kings as by the toiling masses. The tendency is not so much to say simply that humble work, however routine and tedious, is as essential to society as more glamorous jobs, but rather to try to glamorise ordinary manual work. There has been a movement from the image of a 'toiling worker' to a 'Hero of Socialist Labour', with the aim of glamorising intrinsically monotonous work. There are also attempts to enhance the status of lowly work. Technical trade schools seek to enhance the status of labour that has traditionally been held in low esteem by stressing to pupils that it is important to lay out one's tools correctly, to dress appropriately for the job and always to strive to be a credit to the 'noble name' of metal-worker or joiner or the particular trade in question. By such methods the fundamental Soviet egalitarian principle is put across in a way that is indirect, and the various means of trying to make labour appear heroic are somewhat contrived. (This contrasts with the approach of some Chinese Communists, which accepts some work as inevitably dull and, stressing its social significance, requires all, at least in theory, to take their turn at such jobs.) Perhaps in an unintended way Soviet theorists and educationalists here try to give legitimacy to an occupational hierarchy — and to the unequal rewards that go with it.

The fourth principle, the one that promotes study and reward from endeavour, is put across in a far more concrete and systematic way than the egalitarian theme. Education books abound in passages like the following, stressing the need for qualifications:

> The task of the local organs of labour education consists of making every young man and girl aware of the content and historical purpose of the Party and State's appeals and of showing their significance for the victory of communism in our country. Here it must be specially underlined that the truly valuable worker who responds to the requirements of communist construction expressed by the Party and State is the one who has mastered a trade, who has one or two specialisms. In order to build a blast furnace, a mine, an electricity station, a factory or a reinforced concrete bridge, patriotic enthusiasm alone is not enough — also necessary are knowledge and a specialism. [D'yachenko, 1971:203]

This attitude is communicated in the content of the schoolchild's lessons in his reading books, which constantly tell him that his first duty is to study, study, study (as Lenin did). At school there is correspondingly much stress on achievement, with praise, privileges and often material rewards (books or excursions) being given for success. Also, medals are awarded for excellent performance and some grants in higher education provide additional payments consequent on excellent results. Most important of all, perhaps, are tangible monetary rewards that are directly linked to level of skill. Wage payments will be discussed in more detail below (see chapter 5).

A further implication of the fourth principle is that the exhortation to study is couched in patriotic terms. The call to patriotism is a constant feature of Soviet public life, perhaps because its strong traditional and emotional roots give it a force to unify society. At school, on the shop floor, even in the street are displayed banners and posters proclaiming the glory of the Soviet Union, and an element of patriotism is to be found in every situation that is in any way ceremonial or educational. Nor is it neglected in the field of labour education. As a focal virtue of Soviet morality, patriotism is accordingly at the centre of the values and norms connected with work. Hard work is glorified in terms of its contribution to the future communist society, but it is far more frequently promoted as being beneficial to the Soviet Motherland. One of the major mechanisms for nurturing patriotic emotions is the establishment of various *Soviet* traditions. Although we shall be concentrating on these in relation only to industry and to occupational training, they are used in every part of social life. Those that the citizen encounters at the technical trade school or on the shop floor reinforce what he has learnt in other fields of experience.

The Komsomol has as one of its major tasks the education of young people 'in the heroic traditions of revolutionary struggle, according to the examples of the selfless labour of those workers, collective farmers and members of the intelligentsia who have dedicated themselves to the high ideas of Marxism-Leninism' (*XXII s"ezd KPSS, Stenograficheski otchet*, Moscow, 1962, p. 224, quoted by Goncharov, 1972:301). Many Soviet traditions and ceremonies have been cultivated and other traditional ones have been given a specifically Soviet flavour. Old Bolsheviks are honoured in many factories where meetings are arranged between them and young workers. At the Sel'mash plant in Voronezh two old Bolsheviks recounted tales of the revolution in that area and then the evening was rounded off by a choir of old Bolsheviks singing revolutionary songs (Goncharov, 1972:302). This is a fairly typical example of the celebration of a 'revolutionary tradition'. In an article called 'Cultivating Traditions' a writer in the vocational educational press notes that in his school in Odessa the history lessons are particularly utilised — in these attention is paid to the revolutionary traditions of the local working class. Extra-curricular activities strengthen the work carried out in lessons; the local Vocational Educational Centre has a club called 'The Red Carnation' (the flower traditionally laid on war memorials), which has branches in every technical trade school. All these clubs are intended for 'the followers of military, revolutionary and labour traditions' (Tsatsko, 1975:42).

The development of 'work traditions' is particularly relevant to our theme. For instance, the party organisation of the Starooskol'ski mechanical works of the Belgorod *oblast* in 1965 arranged a meeting of three generations. The 'grandfathers' gave the youngsters a banner proclaiming 'Preserve and Multiply the Traditions of the Factory Collective', and a 'book of honour' was installed bearing the names of all the factory's veterans of labour and leading workers (Goncharov, 1972:302). 'Workers' dynasties' (generations of workers from the same family working at the factory) are honoured whenever they arise at a factory. For example, the historian of the Bol'shevik steel works in Leningrad points out with pride how four generations of the Pavlov family have worked at the plant (Rozanov, 1965:483), and this fact is undoubtedly utilised to try to nourish some kind of feeling of continuity among the factory workers and local populace.

Traditions and rituals are fostered or created throughout Soviet life and some are centred around labour ceremonies. The Voronezh excavator works (Komintern) is one of many where pupils from technical trade schools have a ceremony of 'dedication to work'. Each graduate takes an oath, in front of senior workers, 'to be an honest toiler and to live and work in a communist fashion'. After the oath ceremony they are introduced to their future collectives and in the evening there is a celebration at the factory's Palace of Culture at which, to the strains of marching music, the graduates are given banquets by Young Pioneers (i.e. the children's voluntary association) and receive their worker's pass-book from factory veterans (Goncharov, 1972:303).

The creation of such rituals is a deliberate attempt to utilise the psychological effects of the attractions of ceremony and spectacle. All societies create their own ritual dances, parades and so forth to mark events of national significance and *rites de passage*. The Soviet authorities have not dismissed these as petty formalism but have instead quite explicitly created their own alternative ceremonies. Such Soviet ceremonies are particularly remarkable in that they do not limit themselves to marking events in society that are customarily considered historically significant. Certainly they commemorate revolutionary and military deeds just as any nation seems to mark its Bastille or Victory Days. But they also celebrate actions connected with work or the economy in a way that does not have its parallel in other societies — there are, for example, no evenings at modern capitalist firms dedicated to celebrating the high productivity of ordinary workers. Soviet practices try to give dignity and even glamour to everyday life, equating the deeds of mass producers with those of warriors. It is a process that is widely used to romanticise life at the school level and to encourage effort there, but in the Soviet Union the process is extended into adult life — with the aim of sugaring the pill of diligence and encouraging productivity. Productivity is the secondary aim of the creation of such traditions, however. Goncharov, in describing their role, sees them in terms of the encouragement of patriotic sentiments (Goncharov, 1972:300). It is hoped that those who participate in any way will be moved by their spectacle and inspired to feel and also to act in as patriotic a way as those revolutionary, labour and military heroes whose deeds are being revered.

The power of 'traditions' lies not only in their colour and cere-monial effects but also in the undeniably attractive feelings of bonds with the past that they arouse. Many people are given a sense of belonging by the idea that they are part of a constant historical progression. This gives both a personal incentive to play one's part well and a basis for a collective sense of unity — the whole of today's nation shares the same heroic past as symbolised by the traditions. In this way the authorities seek to promote the twin virtues of patriotism and productivity — and particular use of this process is made in industrial enterprises and at schools.

GENDER SOCIALISATION

Closely related to the variance between the egalitarian and the achievement-oriented themes is sex role socialisation in the contem-porary USSR. It is significant that boys and girls at school are often separated for their labour training lessons. It may be that the 'egalitarian' motif is stressed for women and achievement for men. But relatively few jobs are explicitly shown as being closed to girls —

in primary schoolbooks children read of mothers who drive tractors and grandmothers who work as engineers on building sites (O'Dell, 1975:146). Woman's place is certainly not depicted as being only or even primarily in the home. On the other hand, the view of women and work presented to Soviet children is only a modified version, rather than a radically different one, of that encountered in the process of 'bourgeois' socialisation. To put it in terms of Talcott Parsons's distinction between instrumental and expressive roles within marriage, women are taught to help men with their traditional, instrumental functions (earning to provide for the family, etc.); but the expressive functions (such as caring for the health and comfort of the family) are still overwhelmingly the prerogative of the female in Soviet sex role socialisation. In no contemporary stories is the child urged to help the father as well as the mother with the housework and it is always the standard female caring figure to whom he takes his or her tears. Accordingly, at school it is the girls who are taught the domestic arts in labour training lessons and boys who learn basic metalwork or carpentry skills. In this way boys are encouraged to think in terms of a future career, i.e. of achievement, and girls are taught the much more basic household skills that will be appropriate to their later family life regardless of the capacity in which they or their husbands will be working. Moreover, the way in which women are shown to be required to split their lives between two major foci of interest (work and the home) places work in a position of lesser importance than it is for men. Both implicitly and explicitly, therefore, Soviet children are socialised into somewhat differing sex roles, and we shall see in chapter 7 how this affects male and female aspirations and achievements.

It was noted previously that the third and fourth sets of attitudes towards work could conflict with each other, and yet we have seen how each in its different way has an important role to play in the Soviet value system. Obviously the Soviet educational and political elites need to engender attitudes of ambition, of striving and of rewards for the skilled jobs and those requiring qualifications. But for those who do not qualify and who have to fill the unskilled and unpopular jobs, some basis for social adjustment and for self-assurance is necessary. The process by which previously raised levels of ambition are related to lower levels of realisation is called 'cooling out'. In the Soviet Union, Marxism-Leninism provides a useful service in giving prestige to *all kinds* of physical labour and thus from an ideological point of view the 'cooling out' process may not be such a problem of adaptation in the Soviet educational system as it is in the USA (see Hopper, 1971:317). In the process of lowering levels of ambition a greater emphasis on loyalty and on serving the nation may in a comparative cross-national sense be ideologically conducive to the social integration of the unskilled grades of labour. But these have to be seen also in the context of changing wage payments. What does appear obvious to us is that, despite the ambiguities and contradictions of aims, the Soviet worker is subject to a policy of socialisation experiences that is much more consistent and widespread than that experienced by workers in capitalist states, and such socialisation contributes to the integration of the worker into Soviet society which we noted in earlier chapters.

CHAPTER 5

Labour Discipline, Job Choice and Material Rewards

In the foregoing chapters we have defined the kinds of attitudes the authorities would like workers to have to their work. It is much more difficult to measure the effectiveness of such policies. The first value discussed above (in chapter 4) — discipline is necessary for efficient work — may be set against levels of work performance and length of education; we may also study the form and extent of 'infractions of labour discipline'. The question of whether work is a form of 'fulfilment of life' is a much more nebulous one, but some indication may be given by studies of attitudes towards work (see above, chapter 2). The kind of 'respect' in which certain jobs are held and the extent to which education is desired in order to satisfy occupational aspirations may be examined quantitatively by considering the demand for, or the preferability of, different jobs. In this regard, motivation for different types of work is also important. The relationship between qualifications and rewards may be directly studied by a consideration of wage differentials and actual earnings. This chapter we shall divide into three parts: first, the problem of labour discipline and its connection with education is examined; second, we shall consider the preferability or desirability of different occupations, and the criteria of job choice; third we shall consider wage levels, which may exemplify the tenet that workers should be rewarded 'according to their labour'. Discussion of these topics will help show the extent to which the various principles we have discussed have been successfully put across.

WORK DISCIPLINE

There seems to be no doubt that a ten-year secondary education has a positive effect on later work performance (if not always on job satisfaction), and this might suggest that the school labour-training programme successfully inculcates efficient work habits. It cannot be overemphasised that investment in, and development of, education in the Soviet Union is regarded not only as a means of socialisation but also as a stimulus to economic growth and industrial advance.

A seminal paper by Strumilin (1924), published soon after the revolution, pointed out that large economic returns to the economy could be expected from investment in primary and secondary education. Strumilin calculated that for every ruble spent on education (in primary and secondary schools) the annual national income of the country would be increased by at least six rubles (Strumilin, 1957:598). This work has been replicated in more recent times by many writers. Zhamin (1969) has noted that 'Expert evaluations . . . have demonstrated that workers who have nine and ten years of education generally master new techniques twice as quickly as their colleagues who have only six or seven years' (1969:9). Zhamin points out that data collected at a Moscow factory show that speed of advancement through one trade grade is closely correlated with educational background: workers with only five years' education took from five to six years to advance one grade, whereas at the other end of the scale those with ten years' education took only one year (see also study of Chelyabinsk in *Partiya i rabochi klass.*, 1973:131). Even when age is taken into account, workers with nine and ten years education are promoted more quickly than those with seven and eight years (see Table 5.1). Another study by Shkaratan (1970:348) carried out at the Novogroznensk oil refinery showed that, of workers with less than seven years of general education, only 2.8 per cent went up a grade in the course of the year whereas the corresponding figure for those with seven to eight years was 6.9 to 7.5 per cent. A study in one factory of graduates from technical trade schools conducted in the mid-1970s found that they took two to three years to improve their grade compared with the average time of a comparable but non-vocational school group which took four to five years (data given orally at State Committee on Vocational Technical Education).

Empirical work done in Soviet factories also shows that better generally educated workers master new types of work more speedily, and show more initiative in suggesting improvements. It has been

TABLE 5.2 *Time required to advance through one salary grade*
by workers of a toolshop (average number of years)

| Age | Number of years of general education | | | |
| | 7-8 | | 9-10 | |
	Metal-worker	Lathe operator	Metal-worker	Lathe operator
Up to 18	1.4	1.0	0.6	0.8
19-20	2.5	2.0	1.0	1.5
21-25	2.0	2.3	0.7	1.0
26-30	4.0	3.7	1.8	2.0

Source: Zhamin (1969:9)

shown that a worker with ten years of general education learns new techniques two to two-and-a-half times more quickly than his colleague with only five years. Similarly, the equipment he uses suffers from 50 per cent less breakage than that used by the worker with only three years' general education and there is almost 70 per cent less wastage among the goods produced (Kaydalov and Suymenko, 1974:91). Moreover,

the data collected show that among workers with five to six years of education, the average number of innovators who have submitted suggestions to the factory administration was only 2 per cent; among the eighth-grade workers, it was 11 per cent; and among those with ninth- to tenth-grade education, it was 23 per cent. Thus, raising the educational level by one year from sixth through tenth grade results in a 6 per cent average increase in the proportion of innovators. [Zhamin, 1969:10]

Some writers, however, point out that a high level of education does not necessarily lead to greater productivity. Spasibenko showed that of adjusters (requiring high qualifications) only 4.2 per cent had a complete secondary education whereas for machinists the figure was 10.8 per cent (cited by Spasibenko, 1969:125). Spasibenko points out that the educational level of workers may be greater than that required by the level of technology and that this may lead to dissatisfaction (1969:124). On the basis of study in Kharkov, he quantified the effect of education on productivity: he shows that for every year of training up to grade seven there was a 2 per cent rise in the average output. For education after the seventh form there was a slight fall in production. For skilled workers in machine-tool production, length of experience had a greater effect on output than did education — after the initial period of training was over (Spasibenko, 1969: 122-3). As Spasibenko points out, a higher level of general education does not always lead directly to increased production because many industrial tasks are relatively simple; but the effects of a higher level of general education become more pronounced when workers are transferred to more complicated equipment and to automated units (1969:122). It is on conveyor belts and in other monotonous jobs that what Kaydalov and Suymenko term 'the paradox of the "economic harmfulness" of education' comes into play. The lengthening of compulsory education to ten years gives rise to certain problems — a lowering of productivity in the most lowly qualified work, a deficit of labour for some particularly monotonous jobs and rapid turnover among those who do find themselves in such work (Kaydalov and Suymenko, 1974:91).

In the main, however, higher levels of both general and specialist education have a positive effect on productivity. Apart from in the least skilled jobs, labour turnover, infractions of discipline and spoilage of work are lower for better-educated workers (Shirinski, 1973:131; Kaplan, 1969:111; Zhamin, 1969:10). At the Kolomensk Heavy Machine-Tool Plant the proportion of young workers with complete secondary education in 1968 was 38.6 per cent, but they accounted for only 6 per cent of all the infringements of labour discipline committed by all young workers. Khaikin (1969:146-9) analysed the backgrounds of workers involved in rejected production in the Novo-Kramatorski Machine-Tool Factory and found that most of them had only five or six years' education and had been trained on the job by individual or team methods. Another study of workers in two Moscow factories showed that workers trained on the job had on average 6.68 incidents of spoilt production whereas those trained in trade-technical institutions had only 0.8 (Kaplan, 1969:146-7). The cost of spoilage per person was 28.73 rubles for the first group of workers and only 0.45 rubles for the second.

Absenteeism is a measure of morale and commitment, and some evidence indicates that this improves as general educational levels rise. In 1920 the average worker had 23.6 days of absence; this figure rapidly fell through the Stalin period to reach 1.7 days in 1940 and by 1973 it was 0.6 days (Sokol'nikov, 1976:93). At different factories in Siberia studied by Sokol'nikov, absenteeism ranged from 0.45 to 10 per cent (1976:99) and a study in Gorki reported a level of 9 per cent (Podorov, 1976:72). Those who were regularly absent were usually of low education, non-Party and young. (Podorov, however, found quite a high proportion among older workers; 1976:73.)

Several pieces of Soviet research have been done into the backgrounds of young offenders. Tundykov studied 123 young people (under the age of thirty-one) who had been convicted of hooliganism between 1 January and 1 June 1967 in the Kirov district of Sverdlovsk. The misdemeanours committed included insulting members of the factory administration or neighbours, 'physical excesses', using violence, and disruption of the public peace.

The educational background of these offenders was consistently low. Of those about whom the educational background was known (86 of the initial 123), 56 per cent had only four to seven years of education, 25.5 per cent had eight to nine years and 18.5 had ten to eleven. But almost all those who claimed over seven years' education had spent their final years in Schools of Working Youth (i.e. evening classes in general educational subjects provided for workers), and Tundykov adds that 'it is well-known that in most cases the level of training in the school of working youth is lower than in day secondary schools' (Tundykov, 1969:152).

Not only was the offender's educational record short; it was also poor. Many had had to repeat years at school. Of those questioned 94 per cent were not in any way studying at the time of the investigation. The low educational level of infringers of discipline is borne out by other surveys, for example that of Ostroumov, who found that the 36 per cent of the population who have higher and secondary education are convicted of less than a quarter of what would have been their proportional share of acts of hooliganism (Ostroumov, 1968:65).

Another piece of research into labour discipline was carried out in 1966-7 by a team headed by Borisova. This investigation looked at four enterprises in the Tula region and in the Leningrad district of Moscow. The researchers examined the treatment of offenders at these factories and concluded that there should be a correct balance between moral and material stimuli to good behaviour. Most workers, when asked, seemed to feel that moral punishments were more effective than material ones. Despite the very clear feelings by the workers that condemnation at a public meeting or deprivation of one's wage rise are the most effective punishments, about 50 per cent of infringers in the Tula *oblast* factories were punished by a rebuke from the administration. Moreover, those actually condemned at a meeting ranged from only 8 to 16 per cent at the four Tula factories (Borisova, 1968:330). Similar results were obtained in Podorov's survey. He found that the sanctions considered most effective by infringers of labour discipline were appearance before the Comrades' Courts (46.6 per cent of those surveyed), discussion by the workers' meeting (35.3 per cent), non-payment of bonus (35.8 per cent) and movement to a lower level job (15.8 per cent) (Podorov, 1976:76)..

A survey discussed in the journal, *Soviet State and Law,* analysed discipline infringements at two plants into three types:
(a) those relating to reporting for work (lateness, absenteeism, intoxication etc.);
(b) those affecting the work process (ignoring safety or technical precautions);
(c) miscellaneous (petty theft, rudeness etc.).
The results are shown below. Another survey of labour discipline at the Petrovsky bicycle plant in Kharkov over the period 1965-67

Plant	Type of infringement		
	(a)	(b)	(c)
Machine-building plant	43.6	27.4	29.0
Garment factory	45.6	36.5	17.9

(*Sovetskoe gosudarstvo i pravo,* no. 8, August 1968, pp. 40-4; quoted in *CASP,* vol. 1, no. 5, p. 16).

found that as many as 81.1 per cent of infractions of discipline fell into category (a) (*Sotsialisticheski trud,* 1/1969, quoted in *CASP,* vol. II, no. 2, p. 11). On the basis of these data, and judging from frequent newspaper reports, a large proportion of the offences are external to the enterprise rather than a part of the production process.

Alcohol was found to be closely associated with infringements of discipline: 96 per cent of all the acts in Tundykov's survey had been committed under the influence of alcohol.

Another survey of 2806 workers who had infringed labour

Profile of low-lifer

discipline in the motor industry has established that it is men rather than women who have bad records. In the four factories surveyed men averaged from 54 per cent to 56 per cent of the workforce, but they accounted for 92 per cent of those who had infringed discipline (Podorov, 1976:72).

The typical profile of the Soviet young offender would be a man of low educational level, from an 'inadequate' home background and not affiliated to voluntary social organisations; drinking alcoholic beverages would be a major spare time pursuit.

There may then be a minority *sub-culture* among some industrial workers. One piece of research found that such men have few feelings of solidarity with the collective (Podorov, 1976:74); they tend to change their jobs fairly frequently; they are motivated to work more for pecuniary consideration than for interest in their job. In their spare time they drink with friends (42.5 per cent) and play dominoes and cards (28.1 per cent) or do nothing (10.5 per cent) (Podorov, 1976: data based on survey of 2806 workers with poor discipline records). They come from unsatisfactory home backgrounds (only 12.7 per cent of their leisure time is used to play with children, compared with 48.2 per cent for other workers). We would again emphasise the fact that these workers are far from the norm: their dissatisfaction is as much against life in general as against the prevailing political system. Their lower levels of educational attainment are evidence of lack of effective socialisation.

In a more general way, Becker (1956) has pointed out that a semi-socialised personality type develops where the social division of labour is complex and where means of correcting and identifying deviations are absent. This kind of personality type may arise with rapid industrialisation and social change. Hence particularly Soviet institutions such as the Comrades' Court and the *kollektiv* have an important role to play under these conditions as agencies of socialisation.

PREFERABILITY OF VARIOUS OCCUPATIONS

Many surveys have been carried out in the USSR showing pupils' rankings of the 'desirability' of various kinds of jobs, and here we shall briefly note their findings.

Most studies measure the preferability of a given role compared with others; such indexes are closely correlated to the prestige or honour attached to a role. We would draw attention to three such studies of job preferences. One of the most detailed studies (though the sample was small) is that of Vodzinskaya (1973), carried out in Leningrad in the mid-sixties. Secondary school graduates were asked to rank forty occupations according to their creativity, prestige and 'overall attractiveness'. The results, ranking boys and girls separately, are shown in Table 5.2. Omel'yanenko also reports on a survey of pupils from schools throughout the USSR about job preferences. The aggregate rankings ranged from physicists and pilots at the top to public utility workers at the bottom (Omel'yanenko, 1973: 120; *Problemy proforientatsii...*, 1974:166; see also Shubkin, 1970: 280-7). In Estonia, Titma has also carried out extensive research into pupils' prestige ratings of jobs. Rankings on a 5-point scale were: doctor, 4.6; member of creative intelligentsia, 4.5; physicist, 4.3; chemist, 4.25; lawyer, 4.25; mathematician, 4.25; electrical engineer, 4.2; chemical engineer, 4.1; power engineer, 4.1; psychologist, 4.1; philologist, 3.9; construction engineer, 3.9; machine tools engineer, 3.9; economist, 3.8; agronomist, 3.6; pedagogue, 3.6; animal technician, 3.4; land improvement specialist, 3.4; bookkeeper, 3.2 (Titma, 1974:19). (These ratings have been read from a graph and so the final figure may not be totally accurate.)

While the occupations selected and the populations surveyed in the various samples vary, some general conclusions may be drawn. At the top of all lists are jobs requiring higher educational qualifications, what might be called the 'professions' in the West. From the lists we see that scientific interests — mathematicians and physicists, radio engineers — are particularly popular, especially among boys. At the bottom end of the list are unskilled and some non-manual jobs (clerks, sales persons) and those in agriculture.

As the above surveys suggest, the 'mental work' done in a job is clearly an important factor influencing the job's desirability and prestige among schoolchildren. In a study of pupils' job preferences carried out in Ufa and Kazan children were asked to answer the question, 'Which of the following forty jobs enjoys most respect?' Non-manual occupations (chiefly doctors and teachers) headed the list for 77.3 per cent of pupils in Kazan and 86.3 per cent of pupils in Ufa. In Ufa no working trade got even 1 per cent of the votes. The same investigator found similar results when, two years later, he set pupils an essay entitled 'My favourite job': 90.5 per cent chose to

TABLE 5.2 *Distribution of occupations on the scales of attractiveness (preferred selection) (S), creativity (C) and social prestige (P) according to the evaluations of boy and girl graduates of Leningrad's secondary schools (N = 124)*

		Rank					
Occupation		*Boys*			*Girls*		
		S	C	P	S	C	P
(1)	Physicist	1	1	3	2	2	1
(2)	Mathematician	2	4	1	6	4	2
(3)	Radio engineer	3	2	6	5	9	14
(4)	Radio technician	4	5	10	9	13	17
(5)	Scientific worker	5	3	2	3	3	3
(6)	Pilot	6	14	5	4	16	4
(7)	Chemical engineer	7	7	8	10	10	9
(8)	Mechanical engineer	8	10	12	14	15	16
(9)	Geologist	9	11	11	7	6	8
(10)	Physician	10	8	7	1	7	5
(11)	Higher-education teacher	11	12	9	12	11	7
(12)	Philosopher	12	9	13	18	5	11
(13)	Construction engineer	13	13	15	12	12	16
(14)	Metallurgical engineer	14	16	14	15	17	13
(15)	Philologist	15	15	17	11	8	12
(16)	Driver	16	31	27	20	27	25
(17)	Worker in literature and art	17	6	4	8	1	6
(18)	Locksmith	18	20	22	35	30	33
(19)	Shipbuilder	19	16	20	17	20	21
(20)	Automatic equipment setter	20	19	21	27	30	30
(21)	Automatic equipment operator	21	21	24	24	29	28
(22)	Mechanic	22	21	25	30	30	32
(23)	Secondary-school teacher	23	18	16	13	14	10
(24)	Steel founder	24	26	18	30	28	23
(25)	Chemical worker	25	29	31	28	32	26
(26)	Lathe operator	26	30	26	29	31	29
(27)	Railroad worker	27	33	32	28	35	30
(28)	Agronomist	28	21	30	27	19	20
(29)	Installation worker in construction	29	30	31	28	33	31
(30)	Tractor operator,combine operator	30	32	31	37	32	30
(31)	Culture and education worker	31	29	28	21	20	24
(32)	Cook, waiter	32	32	36	32	24	33
(33)	Kindergarten teacher	33	28	23	20	18	19
(34)	Livestock worker	34	33	34	31	28	36
(35)	Housepainter	35	37	37	37	38	37
(36)	Field worker	36	36	36	35	29	34
(37)	Tailor, seamstress	37	27	34	32	23	30
(38)	Clerical worker	38	40	40	38	39	39
(39)	Housing-maintenance worker	39	38	39	40	40	40
(40)	Shop assistant	40	39	35	35	36	38

Source: Vodzinskaya (1973:169-70)

write about non-manual jobs (Aitov, 1966:23). In the Moscow region in 1967-68, over 3000 schoolchildren were asked to rate the attractiveness of sixty jobs. These jobs were then grouped, and it was found that 18.8 per cent of pupils preferred work associated with education, 18.1 per cent chose work in some area of medicine, 11.6 per cent preferred engineering work and 9.8 per cent favoured some kind of intellectual activity not directly linked with production, e.g. translating, archaeology, physics, or biology. Least popular was work in the services sphere, with only 2.1 per cent of the votes, and agricultural work, which accounted for only 3.5 per cent of the votes. Ordinary factory work gained 9.3 per cent of the preferences (Zotova *et al.,* 1970:7). Similarly, 12,500 eighth-year pupils from Leningrad, Khabarovsk and Novgorod were questioned as to their occupational preferences and it was found that the overwhelming majority opted for some kind of non-manual work — only 3.8 per cent chose a purely manual trade (*Komsomol'skaya pravda,* 29 November 1968).

Table 5.2 shows that boys and girls differed in their evaluation of occupations. Gender is indeed a significant factor behind job appraisal and aspiration. If we group boys' and girls' job preferences, as shown in the table, we see that, of the top ten occupations ranked by boys on the general criterion of attractiveness, nine were also in the girls' top ten; the exception was mechanical engineer, ranked fourteenth by girls. At the other end of the scale, of the bottom ten ranked by boys, only two were ranked more highly by girls — worker in culture and education, which came twenty-first, and kindergarten teacher, which was ranked twentieth. The author of the study further analysed the divergence in evaluation of occupations as shown in Table 5.3. Here we see some categorisation of 'masculine' and 'feminine' jobs. While the highest and lowest *groups* of rankings of boys and girls positively evaluate professional jobs and negatively consider jobs in service and agriculture, the boys' list of 'unattractive' occupations includes four jobs that might be considered to involve emotional qualities; dealing with children, dealing with the sick, teaching and medicine; for the girls, 'unattractive' jobs all required work with machines.

These results have been confirmed by Shubkin's study. He showed that boys rate primary-school teaching at 3.7 whereas girls gave it 6.2 on a ten-point scale. The corresponding grades for secondary-school teaching are 4.4 and 6.9, and for general medicine 5.8 and 8.0 (Shubkin, 1971:33). Girls tend to grade even the lowest-status jobs rather more highly than do boys. Unskilled service work is rated at 2.8 by girls but 2.3 by boys. It appears then that girls may be more prepared to accept the lower-status work than boys. To some extent

TABLE 5.3 *Divergence in the evaluations of several occupations according to the criterion of attractiveness (S) given by boys and girls (N = 124)*

		Ranks of occupations on the scale of attractiveness (within the limits of 1-40)				Range of differences (number of places) **
		Boys		Girls		
Occupations		S	E*	S	E*	
(1)	Locksmith	18	2.670	35	1.905	−17
(2)	Mechanic	22	2.661	30	2.381	− 8
(3)	Tractor operator, combine operator	30	1.920	37	1.760	− 7
(4)	Steel founder	24	2.512	30	1.783	− 6
(5)	Mechanical engineer	8	2.866	14	3.257	− 6
(6)	Kindergarten teacher	33	1.201	20	2.862	+13
(7)	Secondary-school teacher	23	2.501	13	2.619	+13
(8)	Physician	10	3.102	1	3.094	+10
(9)	Culture and education worker	31	2.298	21	2.383	+10
(10)	Worker in literature and art	17	3.082	8	2.397	+ 9

* E is a statistical evaluation of entropy that demonstrates the degree of uniformity of the ratings. Complete uniformity exists when E = 0, that is, when all the respondents rate an occupation identically according to the given criterion.

** The plus sign indicates a preferred relation to the occupations by girls, and a minus sign indicates the same for boys.

Source: Vodzinskaya (1973:171)

this less demanding attitude can be seen as coming to terms with the channelling of women into lower-status occupations (see chapter 7 below). Hence, as far as gender is concerned, there occurs a degree of sponsorship, or distribution into the education system and work-force, for reasons other than achievement in open competition. (On the distinction between 'contest' and 'sponsorship', see below, p. 92).

CRITERIA FOR JOB CHOICE

Investigations into job choice have studied the factors that Soviet school-leavers themselves see as determining their preferences. In 1966 in Estonia, Titma investigated the attitudes of 2260 pupils in May, just at the time when pupils were making a serious job choice. The importance that pupils attached to various job characteristics is shown in Table 5.4: 88 per cent expressed a desire to develop their own personality and outlook, and other forms of personal fulfilment

TABLE 5.4 *Pupils' evaluations of various job qualities, Estonia, 1966 (as % of respondents)*

The ideal job should give one the opportunity to:	Evaluation			
	Very important	*Average importance*	*Not important*	*No response*
(1) create and be original	53.5	33.3	7.7	6.5
(2) use personal abilities	75.0	17.5	2.9	4.5
(3) develop personality and outlook	88.0	9.0	0.3	2.5
(4) be useful to economy	48.9	37.9	8.4	4.9
(5) earn well	28.8	58.6	9.3	3.3
(6) be valued by friends and acquaintances	41.5	43.5	10.4	4.6
(7) reach position of importance and prestige in society	8.0	37.4	47.4	7.0
(8) lead people	9.6	27.9	55.9	6.5
(9) ensure stable and peaceful future	20.9	44.5	27.8	6.8

Source: Titma (1969:55)

(rows (1) and (2)) were also highly ranked. More 'collective' motives come low down the list. Titma points out that a narrow form of individual fulfilment may conflict with overall needs of society, and he recommends that educators concerned with vocational guidance make use of strong personal motives (as in rows (1), (2) and (6) of the table) to channel young people into the types of work required by society.

The importance of creativity potential as a motive behind job choice was confirmed by a survey of work attitudes carried out by Zdravomyslov *et al.*, who among other things asked school-leavers to evaluate the relative attractiveness of eighty occupations. The authors analysed the responses in terms of how far job attractiveness correlated with such criteria as social prestige, wages and opportunities for creativity and for raising skill levels. The results bear out Titma's conclusions. Young school-leavers choose jobs that give opportunities for creativity and for raising levels of skill, and that have 'social prestige' and pay good wages — in that order of preference (Zdravomyslov *et al.*, 1970:162).

A survey into the factors attracting school-leavers into particular jobs was undertaken by Gur'yanov and Sekretaryuk in L'vov. Once again, the main motive in selecting seven out of nine occupations in the survey was the level of creativity they were believed to involve. For example, 41 per cent of school-leavers were attracted to book-keeping by its 'creativity' (*sic*) and only 9 per cent by the wages offered. The authors, while pleased that wages assumed so little importance, point out that schoolchildren are not being adequately informed about the real nature of specific occupations. They do not see the creative potential, for example, of jobs on production (Gur'yanov and Sekretaryuk, 1974:19).

MATERIAL REWARDS

In Western capitalist societies, wages figure prominently as an incentive to workers and are an index of social status. The studies cited above indicate that wages are important but not the primary factor in shaping the Soviet worker's desire for a job. But what is the structure of wage rates and the trends of payment, and how in practice are workers 'paid according to their work'?

The fundamental criterion determining the wage paid in state socialist society is the quality and quantity of work done by the worker. Numerous scales and grades of different types of labour in different industries have been worked out. These grades are related to the complexity of work, to its arduous character and to the length of training and qualifications of the worker. In addition various bonuses and piece-work schemes reward workers for efficiency, speed and innovation. Regional differentials seek to reward workers in unpopular areas of harsh conditions — the North and Siberia.

Khrushchev's wage reform, begun in 1956 and completed in 1965, was the first major reorganisation of the wage system since the 1930s, and its aim was 'to rationalise and institutionalise the wage structure which had developed historically but with such alterations as seemed necessary to make the structure of wages conform more closely to current requirements of the economy in relation to current labour market conditions' (Chapman, 1970:16). The reduction of differentials was stressed in policy statements, and encouraged in practice by increasing in 1957 the minimum wage from 27 to 35 rubles a month. The minimum wage rose from 60 rubles per month in 1968 to 70 rubles in 1972 (*Narkhoz 1974*:563). Differentials between skill grades were reduced, and the salaries of ITRs earning over 220 rubles per month have been frozen.

One of the main specific changes was the emphasis on 'technically based norms' for piece-workers — norms based on time-and-motion studies of possible performance rather than on past levels of output. The reform increased the proportion of money paid to time-workers both in basic rates and in bonuses, but decreased the amount paid to piece-workers, as many workers had been transferred to time-work

TABLE 5.5 *The structure of workers' wages in industry as a whole and in particular branches, 1961 and 1971*

Branch	Year	Tariff part of wages %	Payment for over-fulfilling norms %	Bonuses		Other payments, including that for statutory holidays %
				From material incentives fund* %	From wages fund* %	
Industry as a whole	1961	68.1	7.1	—	6.9	17.9
	1971	56.9	10.8	4.8	10.2	17.3
Machine-tools and metalworking	1961	68.9	10.4	—	6.4	14.3
	1971	55.6	15.3	5.2	9.7	14.3
Chemicals	1961	67.6	4.2	—	8.3	19.9
	1971	57.5	7.2	5.9	11.5	17.8
Food	1961	80.6	5.8	—	5.0	8.6
	1971	61.1	6.6	4.9	9.2	11.5
Light industry	1961	78.1	6.2	—	6.1	9.6
	1971	61.8	10.7	5.0	11.3	5.4

*Fund organised in factories after 1965 decree on wages to provide additional material incentives for workers.

Source: Batkaeva (1973:4)

during the reform. As shown in Table 5.5, a much higher proportion of earnings was derived from bonuses in 1971 than in 1961. This, however, is open to abuse and sometimes 'bonuses' become regarded as an automatic addition to wages (Zholkov, 1976:2).

The contemporary Soviet worker's wages then are made up of several different parts. The major part is called the 'tariff wage', and the amount received depends on the 'grade' of work performed by the worker. (Note that a worker's own level of skill and the grading of the work he does may not be the same: see Appendix B.) In addition, he receives bonuses from various factory funds for, say, success in a socialist competition or for introducing new technology (Schroeder, 1972:292) and he receives payment for over-fulfilling his norms of production. Honorific titles also bring material rewards. The Order of the Glory of Work gives a right to 15 per cent higher retirement benefits, preferential treatment in housing, free rail travel, priority of consideration for rest homes and cheap theatre tickets (*Soviet Union 1974-1975:*114).

Each industry has its own tariff-grading system, most allowing for six grades and some for seven or eight. Policy is moving in the direction of all industries adopting a six-grade system. Table 5.6

TABLE 5.6 *Hourly wage rates of workers in enterprises in the chemical industry (kopecks)*

Indicators	Grades					
	I	II	III	IV	V	VI
For work in normal conditions of labour						
For piece-workers	44.7	48.7	53.9	59.6	67.0	76.7
for time-workers	41.8	45.5	50.3	55.7	62.7	71.7
For work in heavy and harmful conditions of labour						
For piece-workers	50.3	54.8	60.6	67.0	75.4	86.3
for time-workers	47.1	51.2	56.6	62.7	70.5	80.7
For work in especially heavy and especially harmful conditions						
For piece-workers	55.7	60.6	67.0	74.2	83.5	95.5
for time-workers	52.1	56.6	62.7	69.3	78.0	89.3

Source: *Khimicheskaya promyshlennost',* 9/1975.

gives the basic piece and time rates in 1975 for workers in the chemical industry (see Chapman, 1970:26 for other scales). It shows that the increases in wages between grades is greater at the higher end of the scale than at the lower.

The composition of a worker's earnings also varies from industry to industry. In 1971, in machine-tools and metalworking, payment for over-fulfilling norms provided on average 15.3 per cent of workers' income, whereas in the food industry it was only 6.6 per cent (Batkaeva, 1973:4). Changes brought about in wage structure by the 1965 decree increased the share that bonuses contributed to the workers' pay packet and reversed the policy of the 1956-65 reform, which had raised the importance of the basic wage in overall earnings. Some bonuses depend on the performance of the shop or section, some on individual output (Chapman, 1970:129-30).

So much then for the structure of wage *rates*, but what of the actual trends in payment? As in Western capitalist countries, differentials in the USSR have fallen over time. In 1932 engineers and technicians earned 2.6 times more than manual workers, and clerical employees 1.5 times more. By 1972 engineers and technicians earned 1.3 times more and clerical employees on average earned only 83 per cent of the wages of manual workers (for more details see Wiles, 1975:31). Table 5.7 shows the dynamics of industrial wage changes, giving the average ruble wage for manual workers over the period 1940-74. (For more details see Bergson, 1944; Kirsch, 1972; Chapman, 1963, 1970.) Here we note a decline in differentials, particularly at the expense of the ITRs. The rate of growth of white-collar wages has been 15 to 20 per cent greater than ITRs' wages since 1960. Manual workers' wages in productive industry lie between those of the two extreme groups, being on average over the period 43 rubles per month less than the earnings of ITRs but 21.5 rubles more than those of white-collar workers. Put another way, the differential between ITRs and manual workers fell from 263:100 in 1932 to 175:100 in 1950, to 126:100 in 1974 (Wiles, 1975:31; *Narkhoz 1974*:562). These data show a general long-run narrowing of differentials over time which we would relate to changes in supply and demand for labour and government policy, which has consistently jacked up the minimum wage and kept down top management and technical salaries.

Table 5.8 illustrates the wage levels of various groups of occupations surveyed in four different localities. The survey in Leningrad was restricted to workers in engineering, but the other three towns

TABLE 5.7 *Growth of average Soviet industrial wages, 1940-74*

	Average wage (in rubles)						Per cent of 1960			Per cent of 1940
	1940	1960	1965	1970	1974	1965	1970	1974	1974
Industrial—production personnel of whom:	34.1	91.6	104.2	133.3	155.5	113.7	145.5	169.7	456.0
Manual workers	32.4	89.9	101.7	130.6	153.9	113.0	145.3	171.2	475.0
Engineering—technical workers (ITRS)	69.6	135.7	148.4	178.0	193.4	109.3	131.2	142.5	277.8
White-collar workers	36.0	73.8	85.8	111.6	126.2	117.6	151.2	171.0	350.5

By 1976, the average industrial wage had risen to 169.5 rubles per month: manual workers 168.2 rubles, ITRS 205.8. rubles, white-collar employees 139.2 rubles. *Narkhoz za 60 let* (1977):472. The average wage for all types of employment was 151.4 rubles in 1976.

Sources: Kokin (1974:16); *Narkhoz 1974:562;* percentage calculations added.

TABLE 5.8 *Average wages of engineering workers in Leningrad and other towns, by occupational groups (rubles per month)*

Group of workers	Leningrad	Rank	Kazan	Rank	Almeteusk	Rank	Menzelinsk	Rank
(1) Management (factory, and government employment)	172.9	1	164.3	1	178.3	1	141.8	2
(2) Non-manual workers in highly qualified technical—scientific jobs (designers)	127.0	3	156.9	2	146.3	2	187.4	1
(3) Qualified non-manual workers (accountants)	109.8	5	111.0	3	111.7	5	106.6	4
(4) Highly qualified workers in jobs with mental and manual functions (tool setters)	129.0	2	97.9	6	115.6	3	119.9	3
(5) Qualified manual workers (fitters, welders)	120.0	4	9.9	4	95.8	6	81.2	6
(6) Semi-skilled manual workers (machine-tool operators)	107.5	6	9.1	5	114.6	4	93.4	5
(7) Non-manual unskilled workers (inspection and office workers)	83.6	8	75.7	7	77.4	7	67.1	7
(8) Unqualified manual workers	97.5	7	73.8	8	62.9	8	57.9	8

Source: Shkaratan (1970:404)

included a wider range of occupational groups. Study of the table shows that the first two highly qualified non-manual occupational groups had the highest ranks for wages — except in Leningrad, where the highly qualified manual/non-manual workers (group (4)) supplanted the highly qualified scientific and technical group. The highest salaries of all are received by the individuals who occupy the top ministerial or party position (see, for example, Matthews, 1972:93, 1975) and are not our concern in this book. It is impossible to ascertain exact levels of income, but here access to other privileges is, in addition, of great importance to the quality of these people's lives. To return to Table 5.8, we see that generally rewards seem to be positively correlated with levels of responsibility and education, qualified non-manual work being more highly rewarded than qualified manual. Exceptional are the earnings of the highly qualified workers in jobs with 'mental and manual functions' (group (4)): this group has high earnings in Leningrad — probably owing to employment opportunities — whereas in Kazan it is quite lowly ranked; also, qualified manual workers (group (5)) and unqualified manuals (group (8)) do rather better in Leningrad than elsewhere. A probable cause of these variations would be the demand and supply of labour in different localities.

The relationship of levels of wages to educational qualifications, kind of occupation and responsibility is generally positive — though there are many exceptions. From Table 5.9 we may note that job seniority, responsibility and initiative, age and skill seniority are all positively correlated with wages. Surprisingly, the only negative correlation is that between education and wages. One must bear in mind, however, that this research was based on young workers, and that many unskilled manual workers are most efficient in their younger years. And outside of industry, data on earned wages of research institute staffs cited by Matthews (1975:8) show that a director may receive 500-700 rubles per month, a professor 325-525 rubles and a junior researcher 105-125 rubles.

Zdravomyslov *et al.* (1970:117) concluded that a varied, responsible, creative job promotes productivity and that, when wages correspond to skill level and work complexity, they also stimulate productivity. But wages were not, in practice, always co-ordinated with job complexity and levels of skills. The investigators found that there was only one ruble difference between the wages of skilled and unskilled machine-tool operators (Zdravomyslov *et al.,* 1970:113).

TABLE 5.9 *Co-efficients of correlation between wages and nine other aspects of the work situation*

Factors included in analysis	Co-efficient of correlation with wages
(1) Responsibility and initiative	0.348
(2) Degree of satisfaction with skill	0.124
(3) Degree of satisfaction with job	0.144
(4) Wages	1
(5) Income per family member	0.194
(6) Skill seniority	0.286
(7) Total job seniority	0.358
(8) Content and character of labour	0.024*
(9) Age	0.267
(10) Education	−0.094

*Co-efficients of correlation insignificant at level of significance of 0.05.

Source: Zdravomyslov *et al.* (1970:393)

Social and civic consciousness (as manifested by party or Komsomol membership, participation in voluntary work and the movement for communist labour) also correlate with a positive and, therefore, productive attitude towards labour (1970:115). The factors that correlate with labour productivity also correlate with job satisfaction. Of particular interest is the fact highlighted by Zdravomyslov that a far higher importance is attached to wages by the least educated workers and that the significance attached to work content rises with each increase in educational level. It was found that the average educational level of those dissatisfied with their work is usually somewhat higher than for workers doing the same job but happy with their work. For example, the average educational level of 'satisfied' machine-tool operators is 8 classes of schooling, whereas for their 'dissatisfied' counterparts it is somewhat higher at 8.7 classes (Zdravomyslov *et al.*, 1970:270). It seems, therefore, as if education may sometimes make young workers more demanding of the work they have to do.

These data confirm Treiman's hypothesis that, as the population becomes more educated and seeks more interesting work, the supply of workers for manual unskilled jobs falls and the prices of these jobs in terms of wages offered rise (Treiman, 1970; see discussion in Wiles, 1975:30-1). There is a tendency, in both capitalist countries and state socialist ones, for wage differentials between manual and non-manual labour to decline. As Aitov (1974:62) has observed, labourers doing manual work are paid higher wages to compensate for the monotony of the work. We would concur with Treiman that achievement mediated through education becomes the most important determinant of occupation and status, and that as industrialisation increases there is a tendency for the wages of manual workers to increase relative to those of non-manuals.

This conclusion is in accordance more with the principle that 'the more one studies the more one contributes to the Motherland'. But the idea that all jobs are 'worthy of respect' would not seem to be congruent with school-leavers' desires for jobs; and, from the point of view of some individuals, incomes do not necessarily relate to the length of study. On the other hand, a compensating factor for those doing 'unpopular' manual jobs is that their remuneration has tended to increase in relation to those doing 'popular' ones. This trend however, seems to us to be not unlike tendencies in advanced capitalist countries.

THE 'PYRAMID OF PREFERENCES' AND THE 'PYRAMID OF REQUIREMENTS'

These conclusions have important implications for the supply of labour to the assortment of occupations required by the economy. Desired jobs do not match up with the supply available, and demand for higher education, in particular, exceeds the supply of places. As *Pravda* has put it, studies of job prestige among schoolchildren show their 'pyramid of preferences' to be at variance with the nation's 'pyramid of requirements' (*Pravda*, 18 June 1971; quoted *CDSP*, vol. 23, no. 34, p. 9).

In considering the overall state of recruitment to vocational schools throughout the USSR, the president of the State Committee on Vocational Technical Education, A. Bulgakov, in an article in *Trud* pointed out with some concern that if trade schools (PTUs) were to admit the planned two million-plus students in September 1975, they would have to carry out considerable propaganda work among schoolchildren (*Trud*, 30 June 1974). In Leningrad the problem has been especially acute. In 1968 the authorities were concerned because the plan allowed for 25,000 PTU entrants whereas only 7300 intended to go either to a PTU or straight to work (*Pravda*, 27 January 1968). A similar shortfall is shown by a survey in Latvia where 20.3 per cent of eighth-class pupils intended to go to a technical trade school in the ninth year, but educational plans required that 24.9 per cent of the age group should enter PTUs — the additional 4.6 per cent would have to be made up of pupils who had had to modify higher educational ambitions (*Shkola i proizvodstvo* 1/71, p. 11 quoted in *ABSEES,* April 1971, p. 13. Complaints about the lack of demand for places have been voiced by N. Rogovsky in *Kommunist,* no. 16, 1976, p. 53; cited in *Radio Liberty Research,* RL 250/77). At the Rozhevsk agricultural school in the Sverdlovsk *oblast* it was found that, of 235 pupils questioned, 170 (72 per cent) had gone there against their will 'under the influence of circumstances' and many were convinced that a serious mistake had been made. Some of them, the Soviet commentator writes, 'found it a great trauma in their personal lives (Shlapak, 1967:17).

The problem of recruitment to PTUs is frequently discussed in the press both in general and in relation to individual schools (see, for example, *Pravda* 6 March 1974). What makes the PTU 'the last resort' for many school-leavers?

Some blame vocational guidance and the character education which youngsters receive both at home and at school. Others [point to] the fact that PTUs offer only a relatively narrow range of trades, many of which are not very interesting. A third group ▰▰▰ers that the fault lies with the status of the PTUs which is still not always very high. [*Pravda,* 25 March 1975]

Schools often receive the brunt of the blame for not promoting enrolment to PTUs. Of 5000 PTU students investigated by the Research Institute of Vocational Training, only 250 had learnt of the existence of their school from their teachers and only 100 had enrolled in it on their teachers' advice (*Komsomol'skaya pravda,* 2 June 1967).

The problem is that often the general secondary school tries to persuade as many pupils as possible to stay on for the ninth class 'instead of conducting vocational guidance in accordance with the interests and abilities of the pupils' (*Izvestiya,* 3 September 1972; quoted in *CDSP,* vol. 24, no. 35, p. 27). The schools have their own plans to fulfil and these lay down that at least such and such a percentage of pupils must stay on into the ninth class (*Izvestiya,* 22 July 1967). To enter a PTU one must get one's documents from the general school authorities. The press has mentioned cases of schools that do not wish to lose good pupils and so refuse to hand over the necessary papers (see, for example, for further details *Izvestiya* 23 July 1971; and Rutkevich and Filippov, 1970:240.) In other schools, parents are upset for the opposite reason. Some schools decide themselves who is to go to the ninth form at the general education school and who is to go to a technical trade school, and many pupils are reluctantly directed to the latter. In Vyborg school no. 76, for example, parents of 119 pupils wanting to stay were told that only 37 of them were to be allowed to (*Izvestiya* 26 May 1974, p. 3; quoted in *CDSP*, vol. 26, no. 21, p. 8). In practice, the pupil does not always have much of a choice after the eighth form.

Approaching the problem not so much from the direction of preference ranking as from investigating whether local needs for manpower will be met, other surveys strikingly highlight this discrepancy between preferences and requirements. When 20,000 tenth-year pupils in Kemerovo province were questioned it was found that only 17.8 per cent intended to take a job, whereas 56 per cent was called for by the plan. In a town in Moscow province in 1970, 976 pupils were surveyed as to their attitudes towards the major twenty-nine occupations of their locality, most of which were trades. It was found that 374 pupils did not find even one of these attractive, whereas as many as 117 pupils wanted to become doctors (*Sovetskaya pedagogika*, July 1972; quoted in *CDSP*, vol. 25, no. 2, p. 14).

The low status of work at the factory extends to some degree even to those jobs open only to graduates from technicums or higher educational institutions. In a study of the life plans of students at various higher educational institutions of the RSFSR, it was found that only 16 per cent planned to work on production. As a professor at Leningrad Polytechnic, A. Grigor'ev, has put it:

> The formula for popularity in choice of profession is very simple — the further from metal, the more popular is the specialism. If one is going to be an engineer, one had better be one in a white collar. [Kulagin, 1974a:120]

A large majority of graduates from higher education are anxious to do research in some form or another 'because they believe that such work is easier than in a factory and in this they are on the whole right' (Kulagin, 1974a:120). Because of this, the USSR is in the curious position of training more engineers than elsewhere in the world but occasionally having to have untrained men (*praktiki*) fulfilling engineering tasks on the shop floor.

It is clear that the majority who wish to carry on with full-time higher education are not going to be able to realise their ambitions. Their disappointment and probable sense of personal defeat can be attributed to the failure of the socialisation process to instil the same respect for physical labour as for study. At some stage a 'cooling out' process is necessary, whereby ambitions are related to actual opportunities, and it is evident that this does not yet happen before the extensive disappointment experienced on failure to enter a higher educational institution. Research done in Krasnodar showed that 80 per cent of school-leavers start work only after they have failed institute entrance examinations (Blyakhman and Shkaratan, 1973:183).

There is not inconsiderable official concern about the situation that has developed. As a Soviet commentator has said:

Unfortunately there still occur instances of a remaining petty bourgeois, haughty attitude towards the working man and workers' job. Also, for a long time, the training system has not been based on preparing pupils for work, on developing in them a taste for manual jobs and a correct understanding of the role of productive labour in communist construction. Some pupils have not wanted to go into productive work, considering it to be almost an insult. Sometimes the young person finds himself in a false position because of the lordly, disdainful attitude to labour which still exists in some families. If he studies badly he is threatened by his parents with: 'If you don't get into a higher educational institution [VUZ] you'll end up in a factory as a worker'. [D'yachenko, 1971:117]

Moreover, many reluctantly forced into factory jobs look on their employment in production as being only temporary, a stop-gap until they find something 'better', preferably a place in higher education (Shirinski, 1973:133). After military service very few are content to return to the same factory and to take up their old trade (Shirinski, 1973:134).

Leningrad sociologists found that 20 per cent of young workers changed their job within their first year of employment (S. Batyshev,

'Vybor oshibok', *Literaturnaya gazeta,* 19 March 1969; quoted by Shirinski, 1973:134. Teckenberg, 1978, has also emphasised high rates of turnover). It could be argued that this rapid turnover testifies to the success of the Soviet educational process in that Soviet pupils have assimilated high expectations regarding labour satisfac- *ᐟ* tion and are consequently reluctant to accept the less rose-tinted reality. Of course, compared with contemporary Western capitalist states, the continual expansion of production and the general shortage of labour in urban areas make possible higher labour turnover than in the West because there is a surplus of jobs — a point underplayed by Teckenberg. We think it likely that the development of processes of 'cooling out', in order to ensure the acceptance of more lowly occupations and of a manual or semi-skilled position in the status hierarchy, may be increasingly necessary to promote stability of the workforce and to ensure high morale. In December 1977, a decree was issued specifying measures to improve labour training in schools. They included increasing the time devoted to labour education in the ninth and tenth grades; increasing the polytechnical and labour orientation of the curriculum; and linking labour education in schools to possibilities in local enterprises (see *Radio Liberty Research,* RL 24/78).

CHAPTER 6

'Cooling-out' Ambition and the Alternative Route

It is widely recognised that one of the major problems facing egalitarian and 'contest' educational systems is to reduce the levels of ambition and motivation of those who are not successful in the competition for scarce educational resources and the more desirable occupations. Soviet educational ideology at the secondary level is essentially egalitarian: it is concerned with educating all to a given level, it is not narrowly vocational, and it has a 'contest' orientation. By 'contest' we mean, following Turner (1961:122), a system of educational competition in which 'elite status is the prize in an open contest and is taken by the aspirant's own efforts'. This mode of mobility may be contrasted with 'sponsorship', in which 'The elite recruits are chosen by the established elite or its agents, and elite status is *given* on the basis of some criterion of supposed merit and cannot be *taken* by any amount of effort or strategy' (1961:122). In practice, modern educational systems contain both of these components; the Soviet system is primarily of the 'contest' type.

A natural consequence of the contest system is that the race continues well into adult life and with the course of time the contestants tire and drop out of the race. They accept that they are beaten by superior competitors or that the costs of staying in outweigh the still distant possible rewards. In the Soviet Union there are many alternative routes for those who are intent on receiving specialised or higher education. Evening school and other forms of part-time study are important ways by which those who initially fail may stay in the race; even if they do not complete their course, they have another chance, and they tend to project failure on themselves — not the system.

The problems noted above arise partly because Soviet work values themselves are contradictory. On the one hand, successful moder-

92

nisation requires a high level of ambition and personal striving. This ensures that an efficient workforce is recruited from the most able strata of the population. On the other hand, the Soviet economy requires that many routine, unskilled and semi-skilled jobs are performed conscientiously. This runs counter to the kinds of ambition that have been nurtured. But an ideology that stresses the usefulness of *all* work and the dignity of manual work to some extent leads manual workers to accept their position in the occupational and status hierarchy. If their earlier ambition is not satisfied they have something to boost their pride.

Turner points out that ideologies legitimating educational structure and processes of occupational and status recruitment are forms of social control. Under the sponsorship mode, control is maintained by inculcating the opinion that the masses are relatively incompetent to manage society. Under the contest mode, the control is more sophisticated and devious. Loyalty to the system is maintained by the feeling that it is not unrealistic for any individual to aspire to success. Hence identification with the values of the elite is maintained until late in life, by which time failure may be perceived but the individual is too committed to the system to rebel. Hopper (1971) has pointed to the problems of managing ambition in the contest mode. It is necessary to develop ambition and future orientation, but it is also necessary to 'cool out' unfulfilled ambition. Hence ambition has to be tempered with an appraisal of reality and the acceptance of failure. The folk norm in the USSR is one of contest mobility, not sponsorship, and individualistic ambition and striving for mobility is a societal value.

There are two ways in which the cooling-out process is developing in the USSR. The first is through the provision of an infinite number of channels for advancement (the alternative route); and the second comprises forms of tempering ambition in the school system — 'vocational guidance' is an important means to this end.

A major means of helping to relate ambition more closely to demand is through vocational guidance at school, and since the late sixties it is clearly becoming one of the most important aspects of the labour training syllabus at the school level (see D'yachenko, 1971, for example). This is a phenomenon of general importance. In Britain, Hordley and Lee have noted the link between early socialisation and vocational education:

Even the most cursory inquiry into [the use of technical colleges and the success of various groups in them] will show that for many young people technical education reflects the continuance of a process of occupational selection and social differentiation which begins at a much earlier point in their careers. [Hordley and Lee, 1970:30]

In the Soviet Union vocational guidance is seen as being able to play a major role in trying to bring together the needs of the individual and those of the state. But often vocational guidance in the Soviet school is not satisfactory at present. When young people were questioned as to the persons (as opposed to the motives) influencing their job choice, teachers were rarely shown to have had a positive influence on their decisions. Schools have a low influence in guiding pupils towards jobs suitable for them and needed by the economy. The highest recognition given to the role of teachers in influencing career choice was reported in a survey of young people in Grodno, where 33 per cent of those surveyed acknowledged their teachers as a prime influence in their job decisions (Gurova, 1973:15). Non-official influences (peer groups, parents) would seem to be far stronger than official channels in the area of vocational guidance (Shirinski, 1973:128).

Schools also have their own reputation to consider. Sometimes pupils are encouraged to enter a higher educational institute by their schools, which thus earn some reflected glory, rather than being helped to choose a suitable if less prestigious trade. In 1966 Rutkevich and Filippov carried out an investigation into the trades that 140 teachers in Nizhni Tagil rated as most desirable for their pupils. Included in the list of thirty occupations, which the teachers were asked to grade on a ten-point scale, were jobs particularly pertinent to Nizhni Tagil. They were asked to grade the occupations according to desirability for boys and girls separately. The results clearly showed that teachers too evaluate intellectual, skilled work more highly than manual labour. The specialists' jobs received the highest average gradings for both boys and girls (8.3 and 6.5 points respectively). Second for boys were working trades (7.3) and for girls white-collar jobs (6.2). In last place for boys came white-collar jobs (4.0) and for girls working trades (3.9) (Rutkevich and Filippov, 1970:236).

'Vocational guidance' is given to those at secondary schools in preparation for entry to the labour market. Not only does it try to recruit to particular branches of the economy, but it also seeks to 'cool out' the ambition of youths who aspire to jobs or training at a higher level. As one specialist on vocational education rather obliquely puts it: the first aim of vocational education is to provide children with positive guidance towards working trades eliminating where possible contradictions between 'the pyramid of preferences' and the 'pyramid of requirements' (Turchenko, 1973:145). In other words, it seeks to legitimate the selection process and placement in the occupational and status hierarchy.

Vocational guidance in the Soviet Union is said to be

aimed at awakening in adolescents an interest in some particular type of work and, on this basis, recommending the choice of a future job in accordance with the demands of the given economic region. [D'yachenko, 1971:9]

Despite the attempts to inculcate a 'positive' attitude to manual work, in practice schoolchildren have only a hazy idea of the nature and demands of various jobs — particularly those at the lower end of the occupational hierarchy.

Because of such 'imperfections' in school vocational guidance, the Moscow Scientific Research Institute of Labour Education and Vocational Studies has organised an office (kabinet) concerned with vocational guidance. It recommends that the school be guided by the following overall scheme for its vocational guidance programme:

Classes 1-4	acquainting pupils with the basic types of work and jobs available;
Classes 5-8	deeper work to ascertain and develop pupils' abilities and interests;
Classes 9-10	broadening pupils' knowledge about jobs and developing a firm interest in their chosen spheres of labour activity.

[Omel'yanenko, 1973:119]

The aim of current vocational guidance work is explicitly 'to make the mass of working occupations more attractive and to instil in the younger generation a greater respect for labour' (Izvestiya, 22 September 1974; quoted in CDSP, vol. 26, no. 38, pp. 23,24).

The above recommendations of the Moscow Institute would imply

a movement to a more 'sponsored' type of educational system in the
USSR, with the allocation to general job areas being carried out in the
fifth to eighth years of the general secondary school and a more
specific choice being made in the final two years. Hence one must
envisage subtle forms of allocation to jobs, of the tempering of
ambition within the unstreamed and egalitarian Soviet general
secondary school. Already some parents in Leningrad have shown
concern because some schools there have taken upon themselves the
task of deciding which pupils are to remain at school after the eighth
grade and which are to transfer to a PTU (*Izvestiya* 26 May 1974;
quoted in *CDSP,* vol. 26, no. 21, p. 8).

We have attempted above to show the seriousness with which
vocational guidance is presently being regarded in the Soviet Union.
It must be noted that there is as yet no one co-ordinating body
linking all work in this field centrally. While writers such as Hopper
(1971:93-4) describe the Soviet educational system as one with
centralised recruitment of pupils, this in fact has been only half true.
It is correct that on the *supply* side the rate of occupational change
and the related of the occupational structure have been, at least to
some extent, centrally determined. But with the exception of the
system of direction of labour and trade training in the wartime
period, the *demand* for occupations has not been centrally controlled.
There has been free competition for places in the occupational
structure: the Soviet Union has had a thoroughgoing 'contest mode'
and students have been encouraged to study and to 'aim for the top'.
In recent years, with the slowing down of the growth of the economy
and of the marginal rate of recruitment to specialist and technical
jobs, the problem has been one of creating demand for, and satisfaction with, trades and other jobs requiring a secondary education.
Greater attention is being given to motivation towards and to recruitment for the technical trade schools. One scholar concerned with the
formation of 'qualified *cadres*' feels that a national interdepartmental
council on vocational guidance should be formed (Batyshev, 1971a:
209). An agency for Lithuania (The Social Institute of Vocational
Guidance) has already been established with the brief to co-ordinate
the work of all the organisations concerned in some way with
vocational guidance (Dagite, 1973:47-8). Thus it seems possible that
work in this field may, in the next few years, become more
systematised and thorough. The implications for the system of social
stratification are that sponsorship may become more pronounced,

that sons will be more likely to take up the same kinds of jobs as their fathers, and that generally the level of ambition of the manual worker strata will be 'realistically' related to occupational possibilities. The other way in which cooling out may occur is through the 'alternative route'.

The 'Alternative Route'

The standard path towards the most preferred jobs in the USSR is becoming, as in advanced capitalist countries, a complete secondary schooling followed by study for a diploma from some kind of higher educational establishment. The contemporary structure of Soviet education, with the provision for technical and trade training, is shown diagrammatically in Figure 6.1. Until the end of the eighth year, educational institutions are not differentiated or segregated. (There are some exceptions, in the form of special schools for the handicapped and those highly gifted in special skills such as ballet. Schools specialising in foreign languages also involve forms of differentiation. Even so, these schools follow a basic syllabus and are unlike the more specialised types of education of the old English elementary and grammar schools — or, at present, of the various 'streams' within the comprehensive school.) After the eight-year school, specialisation takes place and the pupil has a number of choices at the age of fifteen. He does not have to remain at the general secondary school for the ninth to tenth classes, which is the usual course for those who desire higher education. He can instead leave and enter a technicum (*srednee spetsial'noe uchebnoe zavedenie* — secondary specialised educational establishment), or a secondary technical trade school (*srednee professional'noe tekhnicheskoe uchilishche* — SPTU), or a technical trade school (*professional'no-tekhnicheskoe uchilishche* — PTU). [In addition there are trade schools (*professional' nye uchilishcha* — PUS) organised at factories, which provide instruction for a few months (see *Narkhoz 1974*:569). Sales personnel are taught at commercial schools (*torgovye uchilishcha*). There are also special schools for hairdressers (*shkoly parikmakherskogo uchenichestva*). These are ignored in the present work.]

The PTU provides trade training in a skill (or number of skills) over a two-year period; the SPTU combines general education and trade training; while the technicum gives a secondary education with higher specialised qualifications for musicians, medical orderlies, teachers, technologists. If he stays on at the general school, he can, at seventeen, opt to enter a technical school (TU) — equivalent to a PTU — attend a technicum or a higher educational institution, or

Figure 6.1   Soviet educational structure

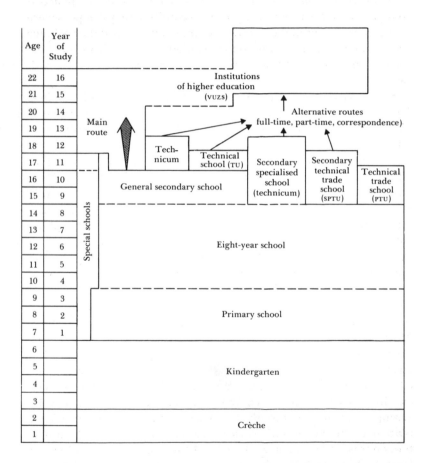

to go directly to work on production. He also has the opportunity to take up additional evening or correspondence study.

Most of these institutions now act as 'alternative routes' and are shown on Figure 6.1. Such routes provide important advantages both for the individual and for society. They give a valuable second chance to those whose ability or ambition develop later in life and to those who are prevented from following the more standard path. From a political point of view, they further societal stability, since those who do not achieve jobs of high-status position are less likely to blame structural features of 'the system' for denying them access to higher education. While aspirations continue they can persevere along one or other of the alternative routes either until they achieve their goal or until their ambition is 'cooled' and they drop out of the race by their own volition. Their failure then is perceived as self-failure.

There is a network of evening and correspondence opportunities for workers to receive their initial training or to raise their trade or general educational qualifications, as well as the more direct routes taking them through training on the job, at a day PTU, or at a technicum. There are also various alternative routes to higher education that are intended for the worker of ability and ambition and are, thus, potentially very significant channels of social mobility.

The first of these alternative routes is through the secondary technical trade school (SPTU), which the Soviet sociologist, Filippov, considers to have a great social significance in the way it opens up the possibility of social mobility (Filippov, 1975:17). It is the ascendant type of school and it provides its students with a complete secondary education as well as vocational training. The general educational qualification entitles graduates of such schools to take the entrance exams for any type of higher educational institution. Most graduates must practise their trade for three years in whatever institution they have been sent to by the labour placement authorities, but thereafter they may choose their own job or may try for higher education. Exceptionally, however, those who have gained good or excellent marks from a secondary technical trade school may be exempted from their three years' work and may try directly for a place in higher or specialised secondary education. The only limitation on this is that not more than 10 per cent of students graduating from such day schools should enter higher education without a period at work (Kuz'min, 1974:84): in practice, from 6.5 per cent to 8 per cent of those who graduate go direct to institutions of higher education.

The secondary technical trade school is a recent innovation in the vocational education system. Previously PTUs did not provide sufficient general education for their graduates to compete in entrance exams, and the current system has not yet been established long enough for any conclusions to be drawn about how successful it is as an alternative route. It would seem, however, that many pupils enter a PTU with the intention of proceeding later on to higher education. 40.8 per cent of students questioned at a metallurgical PTU in Georgia, for example, planned 'to become an engineer', a position requiring higher or specialist secondary education (Kinkadze, 1973:67). Yuri Gagarin is the best known example of a PTU student who took the 'alternative route'. It seems probable that although many PTU pupils might intend to use their course there as a stepping stone to higher education, few would in practice have the ability to compete successfully for places. This is, however, only a hypothesis and cannot be verified until the SPTUs have been in operation for a longer period.

There are other institutions that can help the determined PTU student, or the worker who has gone directly to work after leaving school, to make his way towards a higher education. These consist of various types of evening and correspondence courses. It has already been noted that evening and correspondence training is available at the PTU level. It is, moreover, also available at higher levels, so that workers may obtain a higher education without leave from their work. One study of leavers from a Moscow technical trade school (three to six years after graduating) found that out of eighty students who completed a questionnaire, twenty-four had qualified as engineers. It is probable that such men had enrolled in part-time courses (data given orally at State Committee on Vocational and Technical Education). There is no restriction on how soon a PTU graduate may enrol for an evening or correspondence course (Kuz'min, 1974:84) although it is expected that the course chosen should coincide in some way with the work in which the aspiring evening or correspondence student is already involved. In the academic year 1975-76 there were 2,780,000 students on evening or correspondence courses, constituting over half of the entire student population (*Narkhoz 1975*:684). The quantitative importance of this particular alternative route is in higher education. An incentive for

TABLE 6.1 Social composition of students of Latvian institutions of higher education (VUZS)

Year	Day department				Evening department				Correspondence department			
	Accepted	Manual workers	Non-manual	Collective farmers	Accepted	Manual workers	Non-manual	Collective farmers	Accepted	Manual workers	Non-manual	Collective farmers
1962	3454	37.6	41.4	21.0	778	40.9	54.9	4.2	2330	24.4	58.6	17.0
1963	3556	41.8	38.6	19.6	850	50.7	41.5	7.8	2128	24.2	60.0	15.0
1964	3858	38.2	41.4	20.4	1035	48.5	43.0	8.5	2118	29.8	62.3	7.9
1965	3946	38.5	41.7	19.8	1123	46.1	45.9	8.0	2124	25.8	64.4	9.8
1966	4722	33.4	52.6	14.0	1206	43.8	49.6	6.6	2015	37.0	51.0	12.0
1967	4925	36.6	51.7	11.7	1281	47.2	46.0	6.6	2162	37.9	47.4	14.7
1968	4661	40.3	46.8	12.9	1200	48.7	45.1	6.2	1969	41.8	42.2	16.0
1969	4983	34.3	52.3	13.4	1212	47.5	48.7	3.8	1973	36.6	47.3	16.1
1970	5149	39.9	48.6	11.5	1202	48.9	45.5	5.6	2005	37.3	47.0	15.7

Source: Ashmane (1972:17)

many to do an evening or correspondence course may be the fact that on graduation there is not the same assignment to jobs that there is after graduation from a daytime institution; the young person who is already living in Moscow or Leningrad does not, therefore, run the risk of being sent to somewhere very remote to work.

Evening and correspondence education succeeds to at least some degree in helping groups that are otherwise disadvantaged. Blyakhman and Shkaratan have shown that children from less socially and culturally developed milieux often get their higher education and occupational mobility later than do children of non-manual strata and of qualified workers (Blyakhman and Shkaratan, 1973:179).

As Table 6.1 shows, in its analysis of the composition of students at higher educational institutions in Latvia, evening departments have a consistently higher proportion of students from a working background than do day departments. Rutkevich and Filippov investigated the social background of all students in higher educational establishments in Sverdlovsk in 1968-69. They found that non-manual workers, with 40-60 per cent of students at all forms of higher educational institution, have everywhere more than their proportional share of places, but that they are especially favoured in correspondence courses. Manual workers, on the other hand, have the greatest chances in evening institutions, where they constitute 58.8 per cent of the student population as contrasted to only 43.5 per cent at day departments. Evening education would seem more likely to be an alternative route for manual workers and their children.

The social background of students becomes more differentiated when different courses in various institutions of higher education are considered. Evening courses are effective as alternative routes for workers following applied technical rather than theoretical or arts courses. Workers or their children provide 63 per cent of evening students at Sverdlovsk Polytechnical Institute and 74 per cent at the Mining Institute, whereas they make up only 32.5 per cent of evening law students and 36.6 per cent of all Sverdlovsk evening university students. The figures for collective farmers, on the other hand, show that correspondence courses are a successful alternative route only in relation to the university — at which peasants form 10.2 per cent of all correspondence students. In the other four institutes considered peasants are, if anything, best represented in the daytime divisions.

By the current system of admissions to higher educational establishments, places are biased in favour of those who have at least two years' work experience. The purpose of this is to compensate for the disadvantages in sitting entrance exams to those who have not come straight from a school. Zhuravleva feels that this is a just system for those with work experience who have kept up study habits, but also that it results in a certain proportion of weak students gaining entry solely on the basis of their work experience (Zhuravleva, 1972:188).

In 1969 another measure was introduced to ease the way to entry to higher education for those who had already left school. The Council of Ministers issued a decree pointing out that the work already done to help these late applicants was inadequate and recommending the establishment of 'preparatory departments' at higher educational establishments. These departments would organise courses to prepare participants to the level required for the entry exams. Courses would generally last from eight to ten months and would be provided for day, evening and correspondence students. Particular attention would be paid to improving the general educational level of the students. Those eligible for the courses would be workers, collective farmers and people demobilised from the armed forces who have at least one year's work experience and a complete secondary education behind them. On finishing the course students take entrance examinations, but they do not compete with the other candidates; they sit separate exams at which they only need obtain satisfactory marks (*Izvestiya*, 5 April 1975). They then enter the first year courses, where they follow the normal work of the institute (*Narodnoe obrazovanie*, November 1969, p. 9).

The preparatory departments are used as an added carrot to draw school-leavers into factory work. In writing about the vocational guidance done in schools by the Nizhni Tagil metallurgical combine, its section head says:

> It should be noted that the acquisition of a working trade in no way runs counter to the desire for higher education. On the contrary, it is a positive aid in acquiring such education [for] young workers are sent by the combine to institutes for training, and to the preparatory department when there is a necessity for more fundamental preparation. . . . [*Metallurg*, 12/1975:39-40]

The implication here is that workers who show potential for advancement will be sent by some of the larger plants to preparatory departments. The wording of this passage exemplifies the way in which the existence of these alternative routes is used to soften the blow for those who find themselves reluctantly on the shop floor after leaving shcool.

Preparatory departments do not guarantee their students entry to higher education; they merely aim to compensate somewhat for deficiencies or out-of-dateness in the general educational level of people who wish to enter higher education some time after leaving school. Some research has identified the type of person who has benefited from the establishment of these preparatory divisions. In 1969 preparatory departments were set up at Riga Civil Aviation Institute and at Riga Polytechnic. By June 1970 there were eighty-eight students at the former and ninety-seven at the latter. Study of the age distribution of these students shows that people in their mid-twenties take advantage of the opportunities offered: at the Civil Aviation Institute 77.3 per cent of those on such courses were aged twenty-two to twenty-seven and at the Polytechnic 82.6 per cent (Ivanov, 1972:41). Most students come to preparatory departments with education from ordinary secondary schools — 64.8 per cent at the Civil Aviation Institute and 59.9 per cent at the Polytechnic. It is, however, also of interest to note that evening schools provided 20-22 per cent of preparatory attenders and PTUS 12-17 per cent.

Once the student at a preparatory department has won a place in a higher educational institution he must fulfil the same conditions as other students. Many such students fall by the way-side. It was found that at Voronezh University over half of the first graduates from the preparatory courses had reached the fifth grade of study. For the RSFSR the corresponding proportion was just over one third. At Dagestan University it was one fifth and at the Moscow Machine Tool Construction Institute it was only one sixth. In some institutes, only one half of the preparatory course students reach even the second or third years (*Izvestiya,* 5 April 1975). The social position of applicants may include individuals who hail from a middle-class background and have worked for only a short period of time, and rather than helping genuinely disadvantaged students, opportunity may be exploited by bad students who have been unable to gain entry from school (see discussion in Dobson, 1977:268).

In evening and correspondence courses generally the drop-out rate is higher than in day colleges and the same is true at all levels. In 1972, for example, only 20 per cent of correspondence students actually completed their course and graduated (*Pravda vostoka*, 8 April 1972, quoted in *ABSEES*, July 1972). Correspondence course students have a particularly testing problem in trying to master higher-level curricula relatively unaided, and in many cases they lack access to laboratories and cannot find textbooks. Also, a very high proportion start but soon drop out; in one Sverdlovsk factory a third of all those who began did not survive the first few weeks (Gol'dshteyn, 1973:22). Figures for the Soviet Union for 1971-72 indicate that nearly 25 per cent of evening students dropped out before completing their course (*Komsomol'skaya pravda*, 25 August 1972; quoted in *CDSP*, vol. 24, no. 51, p. 24). In this way their ambition is harmlessly 'cooled-out'.

The system of 'alternative routes' is well developed in the USSR and the benefits they bring are important for the stability of society. The possibility of an alternative route allows the 'contest system' to continue well into adult life; it is a mechanism allowing for the cooling-out of ambition. Eventually, people come to accept that they have been beaten by superior competitors or that the costs of staying in the race outweigh the still distant possible rewards.

Although the 'alternative route' to higher education via the shop floor is ideologically and socially desirable for the Soviet authorities, it gives rise to problems when there is upward mobility for the talented and conscientious worker. Able workers are attracted away from their working occupations. One writer comments that a good young worker with a sound general level of education can cover the entire grade scale in his specialism within six to ten years. The natural next step, if he is ambitious, is the evening technicum or institution of higher education, which 'usually leads him out of the working class, wasting all the knowledge and experience he has built up' (Kulagin, 1974b:160).

At this stage, it may be appropriate to sum up some of the salient facts considered in chapters 5 and 6. It is clear that the process of socialisation of attitudes towards work is uneven in its application. Even so, on the basis of the somewhat fragmented material available, workers are productive, infringements of labour discipline are relatively exceptional, attitudes towards the collective and to work seem to be fairly positive. On the other hand, the situation has many imperfections. There is an ambiguity, even a 'non-antagonistic contradiction', between the different values that the elites seek to inculcate. Stemming from Marxist ideology is the belief that all work is equal in social worth, with a stress on the positive contribution of manual work. Industrial growth, especially in a society that has until recently been predominantly rural with a traditional peasant population, calls for a new type of worker with an outlook of initiative, high levels of skill and a desire to take responsibility. A value system encouraging ambition and striving is called for to meet these needs. In the Soviet Union patriotism, improvement of qualifications and the equality and dignity of labour are all part of the labour ethic. But they are not all equally well internalised as frames of reference for action. The store that is set by qualification predominates; this heightens ambition, which cannot always be satisfied either by the supply of places in higher education or by the supply of non-manual jobs. This incompatibility between preferences and their realisation results in a problem that requires resolution through a process of 'cooling-out'. The authorities seek to influence the status of manual jobs and schoolchildren's preferences for them. Despite overt socialisation and explicit vocational guidance, they have not been able to develop a general desire for a career in manual as opposed to non-manual jobs.

We would add to Treiman's list of hypotheses concerning education and job status that, with the rise of industrialisation, the demand for occupation becomes 'interest-orientated' rather than instrumental. In other words, with rising levels of education people want interesting, clean, white-collar jobs rather than repetitive manual ones, even if the latter are well paid — earnings do not compensate for uninteresting work. We would only partially agree with Matras (1970; cited by Treiman, 1970:222) that the *demand* for occupations has a significant effect on the structure of occupations and on the provision of higher educational facilities. Thus the extreme cases of under-employment of highly educated labour common in developing countries is not a characteristic of the USSR. But one must recognise that it is undoubtedly a fact that many school-leavers want, and many students receive, an education for reasons of personal satisfaction, rather than as a 'training' for a job. Hence the end use of education may result from the supply of various types of labour. Administrative workers receive their education in engineering and the applied sciences. We expect that jobs will also be defined to fit the supply of labour and that large numbers of graduates from higher educational institutions, albeit from applied sciences, will be absorbed into non-manual trades, administration and service occupations.

CHAPTER 7

Social Background to Educational and Occupational Achievement

We have seen earlier that education is becoming more important in placing individuals in the occupational structure. The increasing complexity of technology requires more highly skilled and better trained workers. As a result, the rate of advancement 'on the job' declines and access to educational institutions becomes crucial to the occupational placement of individuals. We may note here that the chances of mobility in 'business' and through 'entrepreneurship' are negligible in the USSR compared with capitalist states, making education both training and social capital for the individual. The demand for higher education is increasing in the Soviet Union, and the number of places in higher educational institutions is not keeping pace with demand. The numbers of students with secondary education have increased in recent years, while the number of places in institutions of higher education has not increased sufficiently to meet the demand of all who are qualified and ambitious. Basic data are shown on Table 7.1. One may note that the number of pupils in the final two years at school increased by over a million between 1970-71 and 1974-75, whereas the total number of students in higher education only increased by under 200,000.

This shortfall in the number of places, together with the great demand for higher education, is behind the increased 'pressure' on entry to higher educational institutions noted by many writers (Matthews, 1975; Lane, 1971; Nove, 1975). Here we shall be concerned to discuss empirical studies that show the accessibility of different forms of education to various social groups. Treiman (1970:221) has suggested three hypotheses concerning the relationship between access to education and industrialisation:

(1) that with industrialisation, fathers' status becomes less directly influential in determining sons' occupational status;

TABLE 7.1 *Number of students in secondary and higher education*

	1922-23	1940-41	1960-61	1965-66	1970-71	1974-75
No. of children in 9th, 10th (and 11th) forms (millions)	—	1.2	1.5	4.8	4.8	5.9
Percentage increase (1940-41 = 100)		100	125	400	400	491
No. of students in vuzs (thousands)						
Day	217	558	1156	1584	2241	2538
Evening		27	245	569	658	632
Correspondence	—	227	995	1708	1682	1581
Total	217	812	2395	3861	4581	4751
Percentage increase (1940-41 = 100)		100	294	475	564	585
Secondary specialist institutions (thousands)	122	975	2060	3659	4388	4478
Percentage increase (1940-41 = 100)		100	211	375	450	459

Based on: Narkhoz 1974:679, 687; Narkhoz 1972:687.

(2) that the more industrialised a society, the greater the direct influence of educational attainment on occupational status;

(3) that the greater the level of industrialisation, the higher the rate of 'exchange' mobility (i.e., the number of positions remains the same but the social origins of the occupants change; whereas in 'structural' mobility the number of positions increases and an inflow of incumbents from other social groups is required).

We shall argue that in the Soviet Union only the second of the above hypotheses is unambiguously true. The first and third hypotheses we would rephrase in order to emphasise that, with industrialisation, parental status has more *indirect* influence on children's occupational status, and that the rate of *internal* stratum recruitment and *upward* movement increases with industrialisation.

PATTERNS OF RECRUITMENT

Accurate comprehensive data on the patterns of recruitment to the workforce and to educational institutions are difficult to find and to evaluate. Compared with the study of most advanced Western societies, our knowledge of the Soviet Union is based on a few local studies; no national study of mobility has been carried out. These studies, however, can be utilised to indicate the pattern of social mobility.

As we noted in chapter 1 above, throughout the Soviet period one of the most striking changes in the social background of workers has been the gradual decline in the initially large recruitment of peasants to industrial occupations and the corresponding growth of self-recruitment within the manual working class.

Data collected in the late 1960s by Rutkevich and Filippov (see Table 7.2 on the social background of workers by age across three generations) show that the grandfathers of all strata came to a very considerable extent (71.0 – 77.8 per cent) from peasant origins. This is indicative of the inflow of peasants to industry in the interwar period. Considering the social position of fathers of the respondents, we note that 42 – 54 per cent were themselves manual workers, illustrating the fact that recruitment was becoming internal to the working class as a whole. The table also shows a slight tendency for greater self-recruitment within the two non-manual categories: 21 per cent of the general white-collar stratum were internally recruited and 45

TABLE 7.2 *Social background of manual and non-manual workers at Woodwork Factory 'Ural', 1967*

Category surveyed	Age of respondent	Social position of father				Social position of grandfather			
		Manual workers	White-collar	Specialists	Peasants/ collective farmers	Manual workers	White-collar	Specialists	Peasants
Manual workers	−20	69.7	6.1	−	24.2	42.9	21.4	−	35.7
	20−25	60.7	3.6	3.6	32.1	18.2	−	−	81.8
	26−35	53.6	8.0	4.8	33.6	31.9	4.3	2.1	61.7
	36−45	50.5	10.3	−	39.2	13.7	2.0	−	84.3
	46+	47.6	2.4	−	50.0	13.3	6.7	−	80.0
	TOTAL	54.0	7.4	2.1	36.5	23.2	5.1	0.7	71.0
White-collar workers	26−35	50.0	50.0	−	−	−	−	−	100.0
	36−45	66.7	−	−	33.3	50.0	−	−	50.0
	46+	22.2	−	−	77.8	25.0	−	−	75.0
	TOTAL	41.7	20.8	−	37.5	22.2	−	−	77.8
Specialists	20−25	−	100.0	−	−	−	50.0	−	50.0
	26−35	46.6	40.0	6.7	6.7	−	14.3	−	85.7
	36−45	50.0	30.0	10.0	10.0	25.0	−	−	75.0
	46+	50.0	25.0	−	25.0	33.3	−	−	66.7
	TOTAL	45.2	38.7	6.4	9.7	15.0	10.0	−	75.0

Source: Rutkevich and Filippov (1970:89)

per cent of the specialists had fathers with non-manual occupations.

Turning to the age structure, we again note a slight tendency towards greater self-recruitment. As the age of the manual worker falls, the proportion of men with manual worker fathers increases; similarly, for the specialists — if we add together the two white-collar groups of fathers — we see that non-manual fathers account for 25 per cent of the over-46 age group, 40 per cent of the 36−45 age group, 47 per cent of the 26−35 group and 100 per cent of the 20−25 group. Obviously, this is a small sample and one cannot extrapolate too much from it.

It is supported, however, by other small-scale surveys. Gordon and Klopov investigated the family origins of workers in Taganrog and found that an increasing proportion of workers were coming from manual working-class backgrounds: of those who entered working life in the 1930s, the proportion was 45−50 per cent; of those who started work in the late 1940s and 1950s it was 60 per cent; and in the 1900s it was 66 per cent (Gordon and Klopov, 1974:12).

Similarly, research done into the social origins of workers at the Chelyabinsk tractor factory found that these varied with the worker's age group. Among workers over 50 who had come to the plant in the 1930s, 51.9 per cent were from the peasantry, whereas among workers aged 16–20 who had joined the factory in the 1970s only 16.8 per cent originated from the peasantry. The proportions of workers coming from other social groups — manual workers, white-collar and non-specialist workers and the intelligentsia — have all increased over time, as is shown in Table 7.3 (Filippov, 1975:16).

TABLE 7.3 *Social origins of workers at Chelyabinsk tractor factory, depending on age, in percentages of age groups*

	Workers over 50; came to factory in 1930s	Workers aged 31-34: came to factory in 1950s	Workers aged 16-20; came to factory in 1970s
From *kolkhoz* peasantry and individual peasants	51.9	24.5	16.8
From manual workers	36.5	56.0	58.1
From white-collar non-specialists	7.8	13.5	16.4
From intelligentsia	2.0	4.5	8.7
Totals	98.2	98.5	100.0

Source: Filippov (1975:16)

OCCUPATIONAL ASPIRATIONS AND ACHIEVEMENTS

The influence of parental status and the extent of 'exchange' mobility may be revealed by studies of educational achievement by various social groups. Parental occupational status influences children's aspirations for education, which in turn affects levels of achievement.

The impact of family background makes itself felt to some extent in children's aspirations for education. Rutkevich and Filippov

(1970:230) have shown that 90−94 per cent of tenth-formers from specialist families in Sverdlovsk intended to study full-time after leaving school, and the large majority of those who planned to go directly to work wished also to study in their spare time − only 1.3− 1.9 per cent of all the children of specialists wanted to start work immediately and to abandon study completely. A low proportion of workers' children also planned to go straight to work: 10−14.4 per cent intended to work and 60.6 per cent planned to study full-time. The children of white-collar families fall in between these two extremes: 66−67 per cent intended to study full-time and 7.9−13.5 per cent to work with no part-time study. The same trends were found in both of the regions of Sverdlovsk that were analysed (Rutkevich and Filippov, 1970:230). In an extensive survey conducted in Novosibirsk and its region, Shubkin (1965) found that children's job aspirations depend to some degree on parental status (this general point has already been noted in chapter 5). This does not mean that children plan simply to follow in their father's occupational footsteps but that, on the whole, they aspire either to a similar level of job or, more commonly, to a job one or two steps higher.

What of the realisation of these ambitions? Generally, social background also influences actual educational achievement. Educational success at school is linked to educational background of parents. Soviet children whose work is unsatisfactory are required to repeat a year. One study in Ufa showed that of parents with higher education, 3 per cent of their children had to repeat, whereas 16 per cent of those with parents with only 1−4 years of education had to do so. At the other end of the scale, 51 per cent of children of parents with higher education received 'excellent' and 'good' marks, compared with 18 per cent of those with parents with only 1−4 years of education. Of students entering the ninth grade of the general school (roughly equivalent to the British sixth-form), 'the share of professionals' children grew by 46 per cent . . . the proportion· coming from skilled manual workers' families declined by 10 per cent, while the share of children of semi-skilled and non-manual personnel fell by 54 per cent' (Vasil'eva, 1973:42; cited by Dobson, 1977:260).

This is reflected in future work. A study conducted in Nizhni Tagil showed that 35.2 per cent of children from manual industrial workers' families became white-collar workers or began studying to

TABLE 7.4 *Social origins and careers of school-leavers, Nizhni Tagil, 1964*

Social origin	Total investigated		became manual workers		Children . . . became white-collar (non-specialist)		studying in vuzs and tecnicums	
	No.	%	No.	%	No.	%	No.	%
From manual workers' family	298	100	193	64.8	51	17.1	54	18.1
From white-collar family (including specialists' families)	168	100	95	56.5	39	23.2	34	20.2
TOTAL	466		288		90		88	

Based on: Rutkevich and Filippov (1970:227).

become specialists after leaving school, as opposed to 43.4 per cent of children from white-collar or specialist homes (Rutkevich and Filippov, 1970:227; see Table 7.4). One Soviet writer commenting on mobility in the town of Sverdlovsk points out that the realisation of life-plans depends more on the material level of the family than do aspirations and adds, 'At the moment of entry to working life . . . more than half the children join the same social groups as their parents' (Ksenofontova, 1972:17-18). As Dobson has forcefully reminded us, many studies show that secondary school graduates with high grades and favourable family circumstances are 'most likely to attend higher educational institutions' whereas those going to work or to a PTU have 'quite the opposite characteristic — unfavourable family circumstances . . . and low grades' (Dobson, 1977:271-2).

At day institutes in the Sverdlovsk region it was found that over 50 per cent of students were of white-collar origin — although this social group accounted for only about 25 per cent of the local population (Filippov, 1974:8). It must be noted that the proportion of collective farmers in the population of the area studied is low (approximately 1—2 per cent) and so their meagre share of students here (3.7—4.9 per cent) cannot be taken as valid for the USSR as a whole, though in fact collective farmers do have lower chances than

TABLE 7.5 *Social composition of students at secondary specialised schools in Sverdlovsk oblast, 1967-68 academic year*

Secondary specialised schools	Social origins					Social position			Place of origin	
	Manual workers	Collective farmers	White-collar (non-specialists)	Specialists	Others	Manual workers	Collective farmers	White-collar employees and specialists	Urban	Rural
	%	%	%	%	%	%	%	%	%	%
Industry	68.3	3.6	13.9	6.8	7.4	95.8	2.8	1.4	90.0	10.0
Construction	65.4	3.9	15.0	7.1	8.6	87.5	—	12.5	90.7	9.3
Transport and communications	76.9	2.1	11.7	0.8	8.5	84.6	7.7	7.7	94.5	5.5
Economics	88.4	1.4	5.3	1.4	3.5	90.5	—	9.5	83.4	16.6
Public health	67.5	3.9	18.4	7.3	2.9	91.8	—	8.2	88.6	11.4
Education	76.7	2.8	12.4	4.6	3.5	70.6	—	29.4	89.7	10.3
Art	25.5	1.1	32.6	36.3	4.5	25.0	—	75.0	100.0	—
TOTAL	70.5	3.1	13.9	6.3	6.2	91.5	1.3	7.2	91.0	9.0

Source: Rutkevich and Filippov (1973:271)

other social groups. A Latvian study shows that the trend is the same in institutes there, with pupils of white-collar origins forming 55.6 per cent and 47.8 per cent of all first-year students in 1960-61 and 1970-71 respectively. However, the manual workers' share of student places has been gradually increasing since 1960: in 1962-63, for example, it was 33.3 per cent; in 1970-71 it was 40.6 per cent. The increase was largely at the expense of pupils from a *kolkhoz* background, whose share fell correspondingly from 17.8 per cent to 11.6 per cent (Ashmane, 1972:15). Hence the data confirm Treiman's first hypothesis that fathers' status has less direct influence on sons' occupation: the influence of fathers' occupation is *indirect* and is mediated by education.

Just as children of white-collar workers predominate in higher educational institutions, workers' children come into their own at the technician level. Table 7.5 shows that in Sverdlovsk *oblast* on average 70 per cent of pupils at a secondary specialised school are from a manual working background and that few children of specialists enter such schools (6.3 per cent of the total, and a very large proportion of such pupils in art schools). The general impression one gets from these figures is not one of 'exchange' mobility, but one of stratum renewal and upward mobility, and hence Treiman's third hypothesis would not appear to be substantiated.

Educational achievement by gender

Not only class but also gender affects one's progress through the Soviet educational system. It would appear at first glance that women have an equal share of Soviet educational facilities, but as one probes more deeply discrepancies become apparent. Table 7.6 shows that since the early 1970s women have been well represented in the specialised secondary schools. But their proportion of the student population varies according to the area of study. Thus in 1974-75 their share was only 34 per cent in agricultural schools but 88 per cent in health, physical culture and sports colleges. From these figures alone it is suggested that women have clearly differentiated occupational expectations in the Soviet Union. However, it must also be noted that, even in those fields where there are fewest women, their share of the student population has grown considerably since 1927-28 — when, for example, they provided only 15 per cent of students in agricultural schools.

The share of women entering technical trade schools was just over

TABLE 7.6 *Women as percentage of students in secondary specialised educational institutions*

	1927-28	1960-61	1969-70	1974-75
All secondary specialised institutions	38	47	54	53
Including in institutions for				
industry, construction, transport				
and communications	9	33	41	40
agriculture	15	38	37	34
economics and law	36	75	83	84
health, physical culture and sport	89	84	87	88
education, the arts and				
cinematography	53	76	81	81

Sources: Vestnik statistiki, 1/1971:90; Zhenshchiny v SSSR (1975:69).

a quarter of all entrants in 1975 (552,000 out of 1.920 million). They were concentrated mainly in apparatus-building, radio and textiles schools.

Kozhamkulov points out that in Kazakhstan in 1970 girls provided only 25.1 per cent of all students admitted to PTUs. Their situation was particularly bad in rural PTUs where they accounted for only 13.9 per cent of admissions. None the less, a significant improvement has been noted since 1965 when girls constituted only 13.7 per cent of admissions to all PTUs and 3.4 per cent to rural schools. The situation in Kazakhstan is atypical in the USSR — it has more women than any other republic occupied solely in housework (Kozhamkulov, 1972:99). Kozhamkulov claims that the main reason for the low rate of female admission to PTUs there is the fact that most 'women's jobs' in Kazakhstan are learnt on the job rather than at a technical trade school. Of all workers trained in the Kazakhstan PTU system in 1970 only 6.1 per cent were trained in 'the narrow circle of jobs which correspond to the nature of woman's work' (Kozhamkulov, 1972:99-100). The author takes for granted that the way to improve women's share of students in Kazakhstan is to increase the number of schools training workers for the textile industry, for catering and other so-called 'female occupations' rather than by expanding the narrow circle of jobs considered appropriate to women.

The position of Soviet women is similar if we consider higher education. Table 7.7 shows that 50 per cent of students in higher education are women, but the proportions range from 32 per cent in

TABLE 7.7 *Women as percentage of students in institutions of higher education*

	1927-28	1960-61	1969-70	1974-75
All vuzs	28	43	48	50
Including in institutions for				
industry, construction, transport				
and communications	13	30	37	40
agriculture	17	27	29	32
economics and law	21	49	60	62
health, physical culture and sport	52	56	55	57
education, the arts and				
cinematography	49	63	66	68

Sources: Vestnik statistiki 1/1971:90; *Zhenshchiny v SSSR* (1975:69).

agricultural institutes to 68 per cent in institutes concerned with education, the arts and cinematography. Women choose health or education institutes, leaving men to fill the majority of places in agricultural and industrial institutions.

There are certain differences between boys' and girls' patterns of studying after leaving school. Vasil'eva (1973), in a study of urban youth, noted that boys are more likely than girls to enter a course of study immediately after leaving school. (Maybe imminent military service for boys stimulates early applications.) Women are more likely than men to begin to study a year or two later, so that by the time five years have elapsed almost equal numbers of men and women are engaged in some form of study. But women study part-time more frequently than do men. Vasil'eva states that 'getting a specialised education entails greater difficulties for girls than for boys' (1973:57) in that they more often combine work with study. She says that this is not explained by any lack of ability or general education on the part of women but by the fact that

a certain number of places in specialised educational establishments are allocated for the study of specifically 'masculine' occupations. Whatever the reasons may be for this, one must acknowledge the fact that women in large towns exercise their equal right to education but that they do so thanks to greater personal efforts than are necessary for men. [Vasil'eva, 1973:58]

Women are slightly more inclined to drop out before completing their course. Of all those who carry on studying in higher education and technicums, 96 per cent of men and 91 per cent of women complete their course (Vasil'eva, 1973:59). The fundamental cause of these discrepancies, in the opinion of Vasil'eva, lies in the nature of attitudes to daily family life. Women expect and are expected to play a far greater role in the running of the home and have much less free time to devote to their own study. To alleviate this situation in the future Vasil'eva recommends better service facilities and a more equitable distribution of duties within the home.

Choice of subjects

Women, as was noted above, tend to choose particular types of courses to attend at educational institutions. Similarly, parents' social position affects not only general decisions as to what kind of school or college to choose but also, if a higher educational institution is chosen, which kind of course to follow there. Tkach's survey of final-year pupils in Sverdlovsk found that technological subjects and mathematical sciences were more attractive to the children of ITRs (44.5 per cent) and white-collar workers (41.3 per cent) than to manual workers' children (30.6 per cent) (Tkach, 1966:61). This is one further aspect of the differential aspirations of manual workers' children. It is generally considered that courses in the humanities do not lead to such high-status jobs. It is, therefore, significant that they are relatively more accessible to children from a working rather than from an intelligentsia background. In an analysis of the Urals State University student population the subjects favoured by working-class students were journalism and philology. Correspondingly, the upper non-manual groups have the highest proportion of students in the departments of physics, mathematics and mechanics and chemistry (with white-collar non-specialists taking the lead in every other faculty except journalism) (Rutkevich and Senyaikova, 1969:52). Since 1966-67 many more schools have offered 'selective' courses and there has been an increase in the number of specialised schools. Dobson has argued that such increasing differentiation of study programmes 'may give added advantages to intelligentsia children, since they are the ones most likely to be enrolled in special classes' (1977:262).

Study of the process of selection to the technical trade schools (PTUs) confirms their low status and often their recruitment of pupils low in the educational and social hierarchies. A story in *Pravda* illustrates the low prestige of the PTU. In this report, an eighth-year pupil has decided after considerable and sensible investigation that he wants to become a fitter and has handed over his documents to the appropriate technical trade school.

> The scandal broke one Sunday breakfast-time. They exchanged good-mornings. Someone said something about occupations and how many thousands there are of them. And Andrey told his parents that he'd handed his papers to the city PTU. His parents intended him to go to a higher educational institution. It didn't matter which but it had to be a higher educational institution.
>
> 'You come from a family of the intelligentsia', his mother said with feeling, 'don't you think we can manage to give you a higher education?'
>
> 'Tomorrow you'll go straight there and fetch your papers back', said his father firmly.
>
> [*Pravda*, 16 March 1975]

Other reports in the press point out that such schools find it difficult to recruit pupils (Myakshina, 1976:2) and during the Ninth Five Year Plan it was reported that 200,000 places on building courses had not been filled (*Komsomol'skaya pravda*, 23 August 1977; cited in *Radio Liberty Research*, RL 250/77:2). The prestige of the PTU varies with the social composition of the area's population. Its standing has been found to be slightly higher among the manual working class (Filippov, 1974:12). For the children of collective farmers and manual workers PTU training tends to represent an added educational achievement, whereas for the non-manual workers it often signifies educational failure. In Nizhni Tagil, a large industrial town, the prestige of PTU education is higher than in places with a larger middle class such as Leningrad or Novosibirsk (see *Izvestiya*, 16 April 1968). In 1971 there were four or five competitors for each place in some PTUs in Nizhni Tagil (Filippov, 1974:12). But even here it was found that 32 per cent of the pupils claiming a desire to enter a PTU admitted that they were not wholly convinced of the correctness of their decision (Petrov and Filippov, 1973:27). In 1968 the entrants to PTUs in Nizhni Tagil were predominantly from the manual working class (84.5 per cent) (Rutkevitch and Filippov, 1970:214). Another group of pupils who particularly favour PTU education are children from villages, and for them the attraction seems to be largely the move to a larger town that this involves. Of school-leavers investigated in one regional urban centre, none planned to enter a vocational school, whereas 30 per cent of school-leavers from the rural schools of the same region hoped to do so (Krylov, 1973:71).

We may confirm Treiman's first hypothesis, that with industrialisation parental status is less directly influential in determining their sons' occupational status; but we would draw attention to the fact that a connection does remain, though it is indirect, and is mediated through education.

We have seen that aspirations vary with social background. From the above data it is evident that the *realisation* of aspirations depends far more consistently on social origins. For each social group, the proportion of those who planned to work was low and was greatly exceeded by the proportion who ended up working: among children whose parents were employed in industry and construction, over three times as many youngsters ended up going directly to work than had planned to do so (Shubkin, 1965:61-2).

The level of educational attainment of parents also affects applicants' chances of successful entry to higher educational institutions. An applicant whose parents have higher education has a 2 in 3 chance of passing entrance exams for higher education; a fellow competitor, both of whose parents have only primary education, has just under a 2 in 5 chance of success.

These are the general principles affecting social mobility in the working class. Let us now turn to consider in more detail the career paths in industrial production.

SOCIAL AND EDUCATIONAL BACKGROUND OF SPECIALISTS AND LEADERS OF PRODUCTION

Treiman's second hypothesis concerns the direct influence of educational attainment on occupational status, and this is confirmed when we examine the educational background of 'specialists'. Data are available for all specialists in employment showing their educational level by age (see Table 7.8). Here we see that over two-thirds of specialists with higher or middle education were under forty. The older men doing specialists' work are predominantly 'practical men'

TABLE 7.8 *Age composition of specialists with higher and middle specialist education, in active employment, 1966*

Age	All specialists	With higher education	With middle specialist education
Under 30	32.3	24.5	37.6
30 – 34	19.7	20.8	18.9
35 – 39	17.1	19.0	15.9
40 – 44	13.9	15.0	13.1
45 – 49	8.1	8.9	7.6
50 – 54	5.1	5.9	4.5
55+	3.8	5.9	2.4

Source: Strana sovetov . . . :233.

(*praktiki*) who have worked their way through the enterprise. Rutkevitch and Filippov in their study of Sverdlovsk workers found (in 1966) that at the Sverdlovsk metal works 'practical men' made up 12.5 per cent of all engineers and 40 per cent of technicians; a third of all 'practical' engineers and nearly a half of all 'practical' technicians did not even have an eight-year education (Rutkevich and Filippov, 1970:184). (See also N. Il'inski *et al.*, 'Inzhener . . .', *Pravda*, 29 June 1966, and V. Akhundov, 'Sovetskie khozyaystvenniki, *Kommunist*, 1965, No. 17, p. 31.)

In the early stages of industrialisation, formal training and educational qualifications were not salient in the recruitment of technicians and specialists; most of the new cadres were 'practical men' trained on the job. With the passage of time, however, training in specialised educational institutions has become a more common mark of the recruitment of technologists and engineers and tends to make success at school a more important criterion for advancement. The proportion of 'practical men' working as technicians or engineers is very rapidly decreasing. In the Novocherkassk electric power plant, for example, the number of 'practical men' acting as designers fell by 40 per cent between 1967 and 1969 (Nor *et al.*, 1972:150). Passing competitive examinations to higher educational institutions has therefore become a more important means, but certainly not the only one, for entry into 'specialist' jobs.

As regards the educational background of engineering-technical workers (ITRs) performing managerial tasks, a survey of those administering machine-tool factories in Leningrad showed that they had an education ranging from only five school classes to complete higher education. The most common type of education was secondary specialised, which had been completed by 34.2 per cent of ITR managers; 29.0 per cent had complete higher education and 8.9 per cent had incomplete higher education. Almost one-fifth, however, had not even a complete secondary education (Blyakhman *et al.,* 1968:178). Blyakhman *et al.* also found that the chief managerial posts were held by men who had slightly less education than other workers doing highly qualified mental work, such as construction engineers. They had ten months less occupational training than the latter group. High educational or top-level occupational background has not been absolutely essential for advancement to the top managerial positions (Blyakhman *et al.,* 1968:44-5).

A study of factory directors in Taganrog showed that a large proportion of present directors had worked their way up through the occupational structure. Characteristic career patterns were:

metalworker → brigade-leader → technician → construction engineer . . . master-craftsman → shift leader → deputy workshop foreman → workshop foreman . . . departmental deputy-head → department head → deputy chief engineer. . . . [Levikov, 1973:31]

The career of the director of the Taganrog combine factory was taken as a typical example. He is Nikolai Vladimirovich Lugay. At sixty years of age, he had spent forty years of his life in the factory, having begun his career there as a turner in 1929. Later he became a master craftsman, then section head, then deputy chief engineer before becoming chief engineer and, finally, director. His life at the factory was interrupted only by military service and completing his higher education (Levikov, 1973:31-2). A similar career pattern was followed by the heads of many other factories, including the Taganrog Dimitrov plant and the First State Ball-Bearing factory in Moscow (Levikov, 1973). Many other directors have similarly risen from the ranks of the workers although they have moved between factories *en route.* The director of the Sverdlov machine-tools group of factories in Leningrad, for example, was a graduate of Taganrog Industrial School in 1912 and worked as a master craftsman in the Kuznetsk area before moving to Leningrad (Kulagin, 1974a:192).

These data confirm the earlier research of E. C. Brown (1966:175), who found that in nineteen factories she visited, fourteen of the managers began work as manual workers. In 1971 it was reported that 'more than half of the directors of the largest enterprises in the country are former workers' (*Leninskoe znamya,* 6 July 1971; cited in *Partiya i rabochi klass...,* 1973:117). Blyakhman and Shkaratan refer to a study of eleven Soviet towns that showed that most 'leaders of production' there began their career as ordinary workers (Blyakhman and Shkaratan, 1973:290). Blyakhman is more specific when he points out that almost three-quarters of the leaders of production *kollektivy* at all levels began their working life as ordinary workers or peasants. Two-thirds of brigade-leaders, three-quarters of master craftsmen and one-half of workshop foremen, section heads and managers began as urban workers; 19 per cent of brigade-leaders, 17 per cent of workshop foremen and 22 per cent of the heads of offices and departments began work as collective or state farmers (Blyakhman *et al.,* 1968:154).

Some interesting facts emerge when managers of factories and large sub-divisions in them are analysed according to the social background of their fathers, rather than seen in terms of the incumbents' first occupation. Compared with more junior personnel, far more managers come from white-collar and far fewer from manual backgrounds. As one ascends the authority pyramid from ordinary worker to manager the proportion of those from working backgrounds steadily falls from 57.0 per cent to 31.5 per cent (see Table 7.9). Correspondingly, the proportion of those from white-collar backgrounds rises from 16.3 per cent — with a slight dip to 13 per cent among brigade-leaders and assistants to master craftsmen — to 41.3 per cent among managers. No such pattern is discernible for those with collective farm origins, who provide from 15 to 27 per cent of each level of worker, including 22.7 per cent of managers of enterprises and the major departments of organisations.

Andrle has analysed the social backgrounds of the 147 industrial directors elected to the Seventh Supreme Soviet (1966). He concludes:

the typical plant director has an engineering degree and, given the attention constantly paid to professional qualifications by the central authorities, the time is not far off when sizeable plant directorships become an exclusive domain of graduates. In the meantime, however, a lack of formal qualifications does not necessarily bar a manager of the pre-war generation from success and national prominence. [Andrle, 1975:150]

Of the 101 cases of graduates, 27 gained degrees as evening or correspondence students, and of the total, 40 — about a third — began work as manual workers. Most (two-thirds) of the directors worked their way up through management. Among the 'post-Stalin' leaders there is a tendency towards a dual-executive role: 50 per cent of directors who started work after Stalin's death had worked in the Party, as distinct from 23 per cent of the sample as a whole (Andrle, 1975:152). The general tendency is for the rise of a professional, specialist manager, rather than the 'front-line warrior' of the Stalin era (see Andrle, 1975:191).

TABLE 7.9 *Workers occupying positions of authority according to social origins of parents (father), as percentage of total*

| Position | Father's social position | | | | |
	Manual worker	Collective farmer	White-collar	Other	Total
Manual worker	57.0	21.9	16.3	4.8	100
Brigade-leader, master-craftsman's assistant	53.9	27.1	13.0	6.0	100
Master-craftsman, section head	50.4	21.9	22.9	4.8	100
Group-leader in office, laboratory	40.9	14.9	22.3	11.9	100
Manager of enterprise, workshop, department, office, laboratory	31.5	22.7	41.3	4.5	100
Other production personnel	44.4	12.5	33.8	9.3	100

Source: Blyakhman *et al.* (1968:153)

WOMEN'S WORK

It was noted above that gender affects educational achievement. And it is when we come to consider woman's place in the Soviet occupational structure that the differential nature of her position makes itself felt even more strongly. Women provide a very large share of the workforce in the Soviet Union: by 1974 it was 51 per cent; and in 1977 ninety per cent of able-bodied women of working age were employed (Lykova, 1977:2). The lack of complete correspondence with women's share of the population (53.7 per cent in 1974) can presumably be largely accounted for by the women lost to the workforce by child-bearing, working on domestic plots, or by the earlier retirement age for women (women officially retire at fifty-five and men at sixty). Few women in the USSR are solely housewives,

TABLE 7.10 *Women as percentage of wage- and salary-earners by sectors of the economy*

	1928	1940	1950	1960	1969	1974
In economy as a whole	24	39	47	47	50.5	51
In industry (production personnel)	26	38	46	45	48	49
In agriculture	24	30	42	41	42	44
of whom, in state farms, subsidiary farms of industrial enterprises, and other farming undertakings	45	34	49	43	43	45
In transport	7	21	28	24	24	24
In communications	28	48	59	64	67	68
In construction (personnel engaged in building and installation)	6	23	33	29	27	29
In trade, public catering, materials and equipment supply and sales, agricultural procurement	19	44	57	66	75	76
In housing, utilities and service industries	22	43	54	53	51	53
In public health, physical culture and social welfare	63	76	84	85	85	84
In education and culture	55	59	69	70	72	72
In the arts	30	39	37	36	42	46
In science and scientific services	40	42	43	42	47	49
In banking and government insurance agencies	38	41	58	68	77	80
In the machinery of public and economic administration, and the management bodies of co-operative and voluntary organisations	19	34	43	51	60	64

Sources: Vestnik statistiki 1/1971:84; *Zhenshchiny v SSSR* (1975:32-3)

although recent Soviet sources on child-upbringing stress much more strongly than before the important role of the mother, with the possible eventual result of decreasing women's share in the labour force.

As with their position in educational institutions, women's part in the workforce varies enormously depending on the branch of activity, again showing the clearly differentiated occupational roles attributed to women in the Soviet Union. Their share of workers is particularly large in the spheres of health and education. Vodzinskaya points out that girls who fail to be admitted to a higher educational institution are most likely to be drawn into work in health or education (or the service sphere), whereas boys in a similar position are more likely to go into industry (Vodzinskaya, 1973:13). Table 7.10 shows that women's proportion of wage- and salary-earners was 84 per cent of workers in public health, physical culture and social welfare in 1974; it was as low as 29 per cent in construction work — inevitable perhaps because of the heavy physical nature of

TABLE 7.11 *Women as percentage of workers in certain branches of industry*

	1932*	1940*	1950	1960	1969	1974
	1 July	1 Nov.	5 May	1 Jan.	1 Jan.	1 Jan.
Industry as a whole	35	43	46	44	48	48
Machinery and metal processing	21	32	40	39	41	42
Pulp and paper	29	49	50	43	49	49
Cement	22	29	37	36	36	N/A
Textiles	68	69	73	72	72	72
Clothing	80	83	86	85	84	86
Leather and fur	41	61	62	64	68	69
Footwear	51	56	63	66		
Food	33	49	51	54	57	58

*Figures are for large-scale industry.

Sources: Vestnik statistiki 1/1971:86; 1974 figures from *Zhenshchiny v SSSR* (1975:38)

this work. More surprising is the fact that women comprise only 46 per cent of workers in the arts. In industry, they almost reach their overall average share of the workforce at 49 per cent but are somewhat below this in agriculture with 41 per cent of the employed labour force.

Most striking, perhaps, are the areas in which women far exceed their proportional share of the workforce, making it clear that there are definite areas of labour activity in the USSR that are considered 'women's work'. These are public health, physical culture and social welfare, banking and government insurance agencies, trade, public catering, equipment sales and supply and agricultural procurement, education and culture, communications and the administration of public, economic and voluntary organisations. In all these areas women's share of the workforce has been steadily growing since 1928. The idea that such jobs as teaching, nursing and office work are particularly suitable for women seems well entrenched.

In Soviet industry, we find once again that participation of women varies depending on the sphere of activity examined. Table 7.11 analyses the proportion of women in eight industries and shows that in 1969 it varied from 36 per cent (in the cement industry) to 84 per cent (in the clothing industry). Industries that were predominantly female in 1932 (i.e. textiles and clothing) have become even more so since then, though women have also increased their share in the male-dominated industries — in 1932 only 22 per cent of workers in the cement industry, for example, were female; in 1969 they accounted for 36 per cent. Throughout the years of Soviet power, woman's place in industry has changed considerably. Thus in 1913, 63 per cent of all women in industry were employed in the textile and clothing industry (*Vestnik statistiki* No. 1, 1971:87). The comparable figure for 1969 is 25 per cent, but this figure has risen from 19 per cent in 1950. Whereas only 2.4 per cent of women in industry in 1913 were employed in machinery and metal processing, 30 per cent were employed there in 1969. The textile industry is still one that predominantly employs women. In 1969 72 per cent of workers in this field in the RSFSR were female. Their share is particularly high in certain branches of the industry — 94.6 per cent of weavers were women, as were 99.9 per cent of twisters, spinners and rollers. Among thread-joiners there were 13,500 women and only four men (Malakhova, 1971:10).

It is clear that women occupy an inferior position in industrial labour. One Soviet sociologist has calculated that in industry there are 2—4 times more women than men in lowly qualified jobs but 1.8 times fewer in highly qualified work, even when many lowly qualified workers are being freed by automation for more skilled work. He writes:

> The liberation of women from heavy labour does not always coincide with their increased employment in more qualified and highly qualified occupations. . . . These jobs are often 'seized' by men even in those cases where the use of female labour has been proved more economically effective. [Sonin, 1972:3]

In an extensive study of workers in Leningrad, Zdravomyslov *et al.* noted a significant correlation between wages and jobs characteristically done by women:

> The class of occupations with a wage level lower than the average includes seven groups with a total of 1506 workers (39 per cent of the total sample). It is made up basically of textile workers, quality control inspectors, assembly line workers in the shoe industry and subsidiary workers in machine-building. Feminine occupations and jobs predominate here. [Zdravomyslov *et al.*, 1970:112]

They show that the occupational group with the highest average wage (113.5 rubles) is that with the lowest proportion of female employees (2.3 per cent). Unskilled heavy manual work is performed by workers with a low level of education, qualifications and work experience, and yet here the average wage is 17 rubles above the average for all the occupations examined. Workers on control panels of automated equipment receive a similarly high wage, and yet they have a high level of education, qualifications and experience. Both areas employ few women (Zdravomyslov, 1970:112).

In industry we can draw attention to a pattern that is repeated in the professions. The proportion of women declines the higher one ascends the authority ladder. Women provide almost one-quarter of master craftsmen in industry but only 9 per cent of directors. Directors of factories in which almost all the employees are female are invariably male. The fact that 26 per cent of heads of offices and sectors are women is explained by the fact that the 'heads of offices' category covers clerical staff who are as traditionally female as they are in the West.

To some extent the clearly sexually differentiated nature of the occupational structure described above is explained by the nature of Soviet domestic life, in which women still play the traditional home-making roles. It is certainly not a result of any inferior general education level. Zdravomyslov *et al.* have shown that the demands of Soviet home life on the woman affect her motives for job choice. Far more men base their choice on job interest (42.2 per cent as opposed to 28.4 per cent of women), whereas over half the women investigated 'chose' their job because circumstances allowed no alternative (54.7 per cent as compared with 43.2 per cent of men). These distinctions are explained by the Soviet authors by the fact that women are far more closely bound to the home than are their menfolk — they must choose work to fit in with their household duties and this often means severe restrictions in terms of working hours or distance that can be travelled.

Socialisation in sexual roles is, moreover, reinforced by the fact that, although Soviet women have the opportunity to do jobs that their grandmothers would never have dreamt of, they still have far less chance of achieving high-status positions than do men. This in itself cannot but be to some extent a bar to women's own aspirations. As we have seen there is much evidence that aspirations are differentiated by sex. Women — although a majority in the Soviet population — are in a sense a 'minority' group with considerably reduced chances of achieving high-status positions. Their expectations are lower than those of men; paid employment does not have the same salience as a career as it has for men. This is because their roles of mother and wife intervene. Their levels of occupational ambition are lower than those of men and their expectations of work are generally more congruent with the kinds of work that are available.

Conclusion

We would conclude that in general terms the role of education in relation to the selection of occupation follows a similar pattern to that in Western industrial countries. There are some peculiarities, however, as far as the Soviet Union is concerned. As Treiman has argued, the father's occupational position is less directly influential on that of his sons. But there is considerable indirect influence: the higher the educational level of the father, the better the chance of access to educational institutions. Education in the Soviet Union is becoming the major determinant of occupational position. This was not so during the period of rapid industrialisation and social change characterising the prewar period, when 'advancement from the bench' was most common. The more developed educational system of the past twenty years is increasingly exerting its demands and criteria over the selection and training of the upper and middle grades of industrial workers. The extent of 'exchange' mobility in the Soviet Union would not appear to be great. While the data available are inadequate to generalise with great certainty, the picture we have formed is one of considerable upward mobility during the periods of rapid industrialisation, mainly in the form of structural mobility. In more recent years, with the decline in the rate of growth of new middle and upper status categories, the rate of structural mobility has declined and a tendency towards stratum renewal has become a feature of the system of social stratification. There appears to be very little downward mobility.

CHAPTER 8

Summary and Conclusions

In this book we have tried to portray the Soviet industrial worker in terms of an ideal type of 'incorporated worker'. We have argued that in many important ways the Soviet working class is more unitary than its counterpart under capitalism. Political and ideological orientations are more congruent with the economic class relations to the means of production. This greater homogeneity has been shaped by the absence in industry of private property, by nationalised state-owned industry, by the role of trade unions and by participation of the working class in the dominant Communist Party.

Though the economic class structure is a unitary one, the working class is stratified. In its evolution it has grown rapidly and has been recruited to a large extent from a peasantry with a low cultural and technical level: until after the Second World War, these men formed the solid base of the manual industrial working class. The 'peasant' origins of the manual worker still influence attitudes towards work, and the socialisation process has been geared towards instilling the desire to work hard and conscientiously. But the rates of economic growth, industrialisation and urbanisation have declined since the 1930s, and this has led to the self-generation of an urban working class. Soviet industry has developed intensively — by increases in labour productivity and a rise of capital stock — and extensively, by adding more labour to capital. This has resulted in a trajectory of economic change somewhat different from that of most capitalist states. While the number of non-manual workers has increased absolutely and proportionally, the number of manual workers, though it increased in absolute terms, has been growing at a much slower rate than that of non-manual workers.

In other respects, the occupational structure has followed the dynamics of the industrialisation process as experienced in Western capitalist states. Following Treiman's (1970) generalisations about the consequences of industrialisation, we see that, as industrialisation has increased, the proportion of the labour force engaged in agriculture has declined and the ratio of non-manual to manual workers has contracted. The Soviet political system has influenced the rate and trajectory of economic and occupational change.

In this context, the occupational differentiation of the workforce is of great importance. Occupation, more than anything else, becomes the key to position in the system of social stratification. Instilling competence becomes a major task of the educational system. It is however not its only concern, and we have seen that the values of the educational system are not perfectly congruent one with another. Since the Soviet system aspires to be socialist, mass equalitarian education is claimed as a major goal and is reflected in the comprehensive and egalitarian primary, and early grades of the secondary schools. Raising *all* to a common level has of necessity to be complemented by the provision of specialised training for a *part* of the labour force. In a developing society, efficient use of resources calls for the selection of pupils most able to benefit from specialised education. Therefore, selection is involved in allocating pupils to different schools. At the same time, ambition has to be raised in order that pupils will strive for the most specialised and demanding jobs and the training that goes with them. To some extent the socialist value of respect for all work comes into conflict with the requirement that rewards are differentiated according to educational background and the kind of work done. In the process of socialisation, egalitarian attitudes are put across in an indirect, even artificial way, whereas individual striving is directly and positively rewarded.

These differences in values, we have argued, have been resolved in practice to the advantage of the attainment of competence and the raising of ambition for higher levels of education and the type of work that goes with them. In the early years of Soviet power, when labour resources had to be drawn from the peasantry, the inculcation of higher levels of ambition and striving was related to the need to attract such men and women into new types of work and ways of working. In the contemporary USSR the requirements of the economy have changed: the rate of creation of new non-manual jobs has declined, and the stock of educated persons has grown. The problem now becomes one of 'cooling out' ambition. With the growing importance of educational institutions as placement agencies, advancement on the job declines. The hypothesis that there less direct parental influence on children's occupational status would appear to be true for the USSR, though we would hasten to add that the occupational status of parents is reflected indirectly, through the educational system, in the occupation of their offspring.

The empirical data we have considered show quite convincingly that the economy's 'pyramid of requirements' is at variance with the population's 'pyramid of preferences'. Some work is more preferred than other work, and school-leavers, with important exceptions, seek 'professional' or white-collar jobs at the expense of manual work. All work may be 'worthy of respect', but in practice not all work is equally respected. Individual ambition, and the desire to develop the personality, take precedence over more collectivist goals. It is recognised that achievement mediated through the educational process is the most important determinant of status and occupation. In addition, demand for education becomes increasingly 'interest-oriented' rather than instrumental: this tendency occurs, rather surprisingly perhaps, in a society where educational resources are purposely geared to meeting the needs of the economy. The political system, in attempting to grapple with this problem, has reacted in many ways. First, gross income differentials between manual and non-manual labour have declined. This process is similar to that in capitalist industrial countries where, as the population becomes better educated, it seeks more interesting work; the supply of workers for manual labour declines and the wages of such jobs rise. Second, levels of ambition are reduced in the schools. Even though the Soviet school system is truly comprehensive (it is unstreamed and all pupils follow a common syllabus), levels of ambition may be 'realistically' related to the kinds of jobs available. A good example of this process is to be found in the differential socialisation of men and women. The latter appear to have lower levels of expectations: girls are less ambitious and more content with lower-status and lower-paid work. This is due partly to the effect of 'woman's two roles' and her higher level of commitment to the family and household. Men's roles are socially defined as instrumental, whereas women's are more expressive. The greater development of vocational guidance may have the effect of guiding children's aspirations along the lines of parents' occupational status: the endorsement of 'workers' dynasties' is a novel and interesting example of this. In this sense then, the educational system is becoming less egalitarian.

A third development is a greater reliance on educational competition. A 'contest' system of educational selection attempts to provide educational opportunity to as wide a group as possible and to prolong the selection process into adult life. Proposals giving access to specialist secondary and higher education to graduates of secondary trade schools will strengthen the already wide network of opportunities (part-time and correspondence facilities) for those who do not qualify through the more orthodox channels. Hence success or failure in the educational system will be 'self-directed': it will be regarded as a positive (or negative) result of the individual's efforts, rather than as having structural causes. The 'cooling out' process therefore is likely to be achieved without any significant disruption of loyalty to the social and political system. Continual rejection in the educational contest system leads the individual to adjust his ambition to what appear to be his or her realistic possibilities. Fourth, one should not underestimate the value that boosts the 'usefulness of all work'. It may provide an ideological alternative by which workers who take the second best are able to legitimate their own position.

While we have drawn attention to some of the ambiguities in the socialisation of values, we must emphasise the fact that the industrial worker is subjected to a pattern of values and beliefs that is consistently and persistently transmitted. The educational system is a leading part of the 'ideological state apparatus', and socialisation is the main agent ensuring political reliability. Political socialisation has been overt in the Soviet Union because the school system has been called upon to change people's beliefs. As new beliefs become internalised and come to be 'taken for granted', it seems likely that the procedures of formal socialisation will become redundant and we would expect such methods to decline. In the school there is a very strong boundary between what knowledge may and may not be transmitted. Subjects have little autonomy, and the 'professionalisation' of trades through unions hardly exists.

As at the place of work, the activity of integrating the members of the institution and of linking the institution to the wider society is carried out by the political party and the trade union. The institutional arrangements are not as centralised and uniform as many commentators have assumed. At the industrial enterprise, we have suggested, the organisational structure departs from the hierarchical arrangement of a bureaucracy suggested by Weber. There is a plurality of institutions all having separate links with superior independent external bodies: industrial ministry, Party, trade union, organs of People's Control. These agencies operate to try to ensure that 'substantive' rather than 'instrumental' rationality prevails, and they also operate to involve or mobilise workers in the activity of the factory.

The process of socialisation and the institutional structure serve to integrate workers fairly successfully into the system. If we regard alienation to be structurally conditioned by (property) class exploitation, then it is absent in the USSR. But other forms of alienation are evident: they express themselves in dissatisfaction with, and instrumental attitudes to, work and in feelings of powerlessness. At root, we believe, this is because the Soviet Union is a transitional society, in which the state rules on behalf of the working class. Workers have no direct control over the means of production and this is a cause of some forms of disaffection. To this extent, the Soviet working class is not a class 'for itself'.

But Soviet workers, as we have seen, do have various forms of participation that help to integrate them into the industrial enterprise. In this respect, the working class is socially and politically stratified, and there are some workers with a low level of allegiance to the *kollektiv*. The most 'dissatisfied' group of workers with respect to attitude towards work, towards socialist property, and towards social activity are unskilled manual workers with low levels of education. Another dissatisfied group are those whose education and qualifications are superior to the kind of work that they do. We reject the notion that they are part of a 'counter-culture'; rather we see them as members of a sub-cultural group discontented with certain arrangements or 'outputs' of the Soviet system. On the whole, within the context of the state system, levels of participation of workers in the Party and in the production process in the Soviet factory are high; they serve to create a sense of involvement and, particularly through the Party, provide forms of political 'inputs'. Again, various groups of workers participate differentially: the better educated, more highly qualified are likely to be members of the Party and to take part in the voluntary activities organised in the factory.

There are then forms of structural and social integration that act as constraints on the industrial worker. These operate to create what we have termed an 'incorporated' worker. We have rejected the types of the 'traditional', 'deferential' and 'privatised' worker. The Soviet worker does share with the 'traditional' worker closely knit networks of friendship and social activity at the place of work: even more so because, unlike under modern Western capitalism, the ruling political party is firmly lodged at the industrial enterprise. Unlike the traditional worker, the Soviet worker's life-style is directly fostered by the factory and has not developed in opposition to it: his values and beliefs do not form part of a counter-culture. Similarly to the 'deferential' worker the Soviet worker is brought into close association with employees and other 'middle-class influentials', but he does not regard management as a kind of ascriptive elite; there are high levels of mobility, and the distance between management and worker (between 'staff' and 'works') is very much less than in this model. The typology of the 'privatised' worker does not fit the Soviet worker. The trade union is not a 'utilitarian association for raising the worker's standard of living', and Soviet Marxism-Leninism does not sustain a 'pecuniary model of society': not yet. There are sub-cultures, it is true, in which work is regarded as instrumental and the wage packet is of greatest importance. Also, wage incentives are becoming more important and would appear to be likely to increase. But these tendencies do not add up to what is referred to as a 'privatised' worker. An 'incorporated' worker is an 'ideal' type: he accepts the authority structure of the industrial enterprise, he actively participates in the improvement of production and for him the factory is a focus of political and social life. Such a worker is closer to the values of the factory administration than the capitalist worker. He shares a general concern to promote the 'national interest'. Acceptance of the factory system entails acceptance of the whole social system: to work for the improvement of the enterprise is to work for the improvement of the Soviet system. The worker is part of a contest educational system that leads to the social, occupational and political advancement of the ambitious worker. Even if he has aspired in childhood and youth to a higher education and a job that is commensurate with it, Soviet ideology provides some compensation for the manual worker: it gives a place of honour to all forms of physical labour. While we do not envisage any major forms of systemic conflict, it is more likely that, if the 'pragmatic' expectations concerning improvement of living standards (considered in their widest sense) are not met, then dissatisfaction is likely to mount. 'Aspirational deprivation', where consumer demands rise and supply does not increase to meet it, resulting in shortages of goods, seems a likely development; and social tension may well rise as a response to inadequate economic performance. Even so, the effects of socialisation and the institutional structure of the Soviet industrial enterprise will, we believe, be sufficient to accommodate the kinds of economistic demands likely to be articulated by the contemporary Soviet worker.

The Administration of a Technical Trade School

In this appendix we shall situate the process of labour education in its institutional setting. We shall consider the various institutional groupings at the technical trade school. In both the schools and the industrial enterprise there are formal representatives of the administration (the school director and the factory chief), of the Party and of the trade union, and there are in addition other voluntary groupings. In chapter 2 we described the institutional structure of the Soviet industrial enterprise; here we shall be concerned with the parallel features of the institutions that train the worker. We shall see that the structural arrangement attempts to ensure that the requirements of society, *as defined by its elites*, are directly transmitted through the educational system and that various other interests (pupils', parents', teachers', trades', professions') may not frustrate or control these demands. In a way that is more direct than in the West, social control, economic needs and awareness of general political values are explicit both in the curriculum and in the control of educational institutions.

At the head of the staff is the director. He co-ordinates all the bodies in any way connected with the school, e.g. teaching staff, parents, base enterprise, and the State Committee on Vocational Technical Education. In addition to his co-ordinating function, his other main role is supervising. He observes the teachers by regularly inspecting lessons and he oversees many student after-school activities: he is kept well informed of meetings of the Young Communist League, which he may attend. He also is responsible for the enforcement of school discipline. The director is one of several agencies that regularly check that the authorities' education syllabuses and guidelines are adhered to by the teaching staff (Makienko *et al.*, 1971:226-7).

The *pedagogical council* is one of the institution's most important bodies and has as its general aim the improvement of the teaching process. It consists not only of the teaching staff but also of the librarian, the military education officers, the school's doctor and representatives of social organisations, the parents' council and the base enterprise. In other words, anyone who has an interest at all in the work of the school can voice his views to the council — though students are not formally represented. The council should meet at least once a month and works according to a plan that covers each year or half-year. As well as discussing methods of improving education in the school, the council is also concerned with ways of increasing work efficiency (NOT — *nauchnaya organizatsiya truda;* literally, scientific organisation of labour, i.e. work efficiency) and planning (Makienko *et al.,* 1971:200-10). The pedagogical council also works out demands to be made on the teaching staff. At the Nizhni Tagil mining-metallurgical trades school, for example, every teacher has his own schedule for the period of the next five-year plan which involves raising his specialist, pedagogical and political qualifications (Borisov, 1974:8).

Another important institution of the technical trade school is the *methods commission.* One of these is created for each area of study; for example, there will be in some institutions a methods commission for carpentry or brick-laying trades. Methods commissions are also created for each related group of technical or general educational subjects — there are subject methods commissions on technical drawing and social sciences — which are made up of the staff involved in the particular field.

The work of the *parents' council* is broad but again has a special relevance to the character-education aspect of the life of the school. Its activities include members' keeping an eye on the appearance and dress of pupils (when there are 'inadequacies' here contact is made with the offender's parents), organising discussions on such themes as the international situation, the harmful effects of smoking or the nature of cultured behaviour, and summoning to the council individual pupils (and their parents) who have infringed discipline or whose behaviour is felt to deserve particular commendation. It also helps the trade union in organising parents to prepare New Year presents for orphan pupils and to arrange holidays for them with families (Makienko *et al,* 1971:211).

Having noted these agencies that involve teachers, parents and, to a lesser degree, pupils in the running of the school, it is perhaps important to stress the fact that the 'frame' or context in which knowledge is transmitted is inflexible in the sense that neither teacher nor pupil is able to control what is taught. Here the pedagogical relationship is bonded by social and moral demands: the institutions of the school seek to integrate the pedagogical with the social and political. To ensure this strong bondage numerous institutions in the technical trade school have oversight over the process of socialisation.

As was mentioned above, the director of the school is but one of several people involved in ascertaining that the institution is carrying out its work satisfactorily. The main methods of inspection are carried out by the teachers themselves. Master-craftsmen and teachers visit each others' lessons, analysing them and discussing them 'with a comradely exchange of experience'. The Soviet use of collective criticism from early school age has doubtless accustomed their teachers to the idea of such a form of monitoring. A slightly more formal development of this method of inspection is organised by the pedagogical council. This keeps a general running check on the quality of the work done by each individual master-craftsman and teacher in order to ascertain how conscientiously and precisely he is fulfilling his duties and to see where help is particularly needed. Each teacher or craftsman should be visited once every six months and those who have shown inadequacies should be visited more frequently (Makienko *et al.*, 1971:228).

The pedagogical council also carries out inspections on the basis of examining various teachers' presentations of the same topic to different groups. Results from each group are compared and conclusions drawn with the aim of helping teachers to improve their approach in future years (Makienko *et al.*, 1971:229). An extensive programme of inspection of the teachers of labour training in Byelorussian schools was carried out in 1971 when 3480 master-craftsmen were observed. Not all successfully passed the inspection: 78 were replaced, 20 had to take a second test and 400 were advised to do some study in their spare time (Shantrukova, 1974:49). The custom of inspecting lessons in the Soviet Union allows a constant check on teachers' work, and must do much to make teachers present things in the ways favoured by the authorities.

POLITICAL ORGANISATIONS IN THE TECHNICAL TRADE SCHOOL

All the major Soviet political organisations (the Komsomol, the Party and the appropriate industrial trade union) have branches in the trade school. The Komsomol is fairly closely guided by the director and the teaching staff. Its role is defined as helping the teaching staff to improve educational work. It seeks to instil the moral qualities of Soviet patriotism, collectivism, discipline and a communist attitude to labour (Makienko *et al.*, 1971:213). In a technical trade school the Komsomol organisation has features differentiating it from its sister branch in a factory: its composition is predominantly young; many students are not members when they arrive and must be brought into the organisation; and it also has a very rapidly changing membership.

All teaching staff, whether they are Komsomol members or not, are encouraged to take part in its meetings. The stated aim of this is to 'enrich and strengthen the Komsomol's work' (Makienko *et al.*, 1971:214) but in rather more specific language it acts to guide decisions and to check behaviour. The typical Komsomol group will participate in all major areas of the school's life — admissions, curriculum planning, organisation of practical work and subsequent use of graduates on production. Sometimes it will spend much time on vocational guidance work by organising exhibitions and information sessions at the schools and regularly arranging Open Days.

The Komsomol is also concerned in technical trade schools with military training. The secretary of the Komsomol committee, along with Party and trade union representatives and members of staff with particular responsibilities for military and physical education, form a council to deal with the 'military—patriotic training' of pupils.

In addition to the Komsomol, every institution has its 'pupils *aktiv*' — student representatives with particular organisational responsibi-lities. The particular focus of the pupils' *aktiv* is in fostering a sense of collectivism which, in the Soviet context, implies a leader or group of leaders; the collective here is led by its *aktiv*. The main members of this are the leader (*starosta*), the Komsomol secretary and the trade union group organiser (*profgruporg*). There is thus no chance of the pupils' collective articulating views in the opposition to the dominant social—political organisations (Komsomol, Party, trade union).

The group leader has the most important part to play in the running of the pupils' collective. He is chosen at a group meeting on the basis of the recommendation of the master-craftsman of the group and his appointment has to be ratified by the director himself. All members of the admissions' commission must make notes on each pupil, and it is on the basis of this information that the group leader will be selected (Makienko *et al.*, 1971:216). Every attempt will be made to choose, from the leadership's viewpoint, the most socially responsible, committed and hard-working person available.

These organisations may be regarded as instruments to help the teaching staff rather than to protect the rights of students when these occasionally clash with those of the staff. Soviet texts use the term 'student self-administration' to describe the students' collective and the Komsomol organisation in the school, but it is a very different concept from that advocated by its contemporary Western adherents. In the Soviet Union the ideology of the elites seeks to bind individuals to the collective, and 'self-administration' takes place in this context. This activity helps accustom school pupils to do voluntary work.

The Party organisation in the technical trade schools deals much more with the teaching staff than with the pupils. It is clearly the main channel of Party policy in the institution, and the director is said to take decisions with the aid of the Party organisation. It is concerned with political propagandist work among the staff but it also has a particular responsibility towards guiding the Komsomol (Makienko *et al.*, 1971:213).

Once he joins a trade school a pupil may become a member of a trade union. The trade union organisation of the teaching staff must explain the trade union's goals, its structure, laws and members' duties to all new pupils. The trade union organisation is very active in the technical trade school and all pupils are encouraged to join. The union's tasks in relation to the school are to raise the quality of pupils' creative activity, especially by organising socialist competitions; to help in the provision of consumer services for pupils, looking after questions of hygiene, catering and health; and to help in the political and cultural education of pupils and in the development of sport (Makienko *et al.*, 1971:215).

We might suggest that Makienko presents the trade union in the school as an interest group when he says that it must work 'to improve conditions of work and daily life for the pupils' (Makienko *et al.*, 1971:215). But the trade union is far from being a counter to the interests of the authorities; it has to work with, and for, the leadership of the school and in the terms of the prescribed values and norms. The role of the trade union in vocational education is supportive. Its aim is not to express a conflicting point of view to the other bodies involved, and it would not see itself as defending a particular 'interest group' from potential abuse. Its main tasks are: to see that all the places planned in educational institutions in practice become available as required; to see that the institutes training in various specialisms have adequate facilities; and to check that the type of training received is most relevant to the work that students will have to do in the future.

There are, to sum up, four main features characterising the work of the trade union at the technical trade school: it is supportive of the work done by other organisations; it tends to have a positively practical role; it has an important socialising role; and it provides an integrating mechanism, giving young people a sense of belonging. Just like the institutional setup described in chapter 2, the arrangements of the vocational school work systematically to incorporate the pupil.

Training at the Place of Work

Despite the attention given to the formal educational process in the USSR, trade training directly at the place of work is still, in terms of the numbers of workers trained, by far the more important means of training. Table A1 shows that the majority of workers are still trained on the job. Thus, well over three-quarters of workers in 1965 were trained directly on production, though the proportion varies according to the branch of the economy. Only in agriculture are more workers trained in schools than directly on the farm. In industry in 1971 nearly six times as many skilled workers were trained on the job at the enterprise than in the formal educational system. Since 1965, there has been an increase in the number of workers trained in educational institutions, but these still account for only just over one-quarter of all workers, including those in agriculture. The proportion of workers trained on production is slowly decreasing, but the absolute number of workers trained here has increased from between 3.4 million in 1965 to 5.6 million in 1974.

TABLE A1   *The ratio of qualified workers trained in the system of vocational education to the number trained directly on the job (system of vocational education taken as the unit)*

Branch of the economy	1965	1969	1971
Industry	1:8.3	1:6.4	1:5.7
Construction	1:2.5	1:2.5	1:2.7
Agriculture	1:0.6	1:0.5	1:0.5
Transport	1:9.3	1:6.2	1:5.7

Source: Omel'yanenko (1973:109)

We may distinguish between three different modes of training of workers on production:
(1) initial training of new workers;
(2) re-training in a new specialism; and

145

(3) raising of previous qualifications.

The organisational structure of production training is laid down in a Model Statute drawn up in October 1968. This says that the new worker's initial training is to be (1) individual, or (2) brigade, or (3) coursework (with or without day release). The most important, as far as the number of workers trained is concerned, is *individual* on-the-job training, which in 1966 accounted for 71.3 per cent of workers trained on production (Novgorodski and Khaykin, 1968:14). This method of training is a process whereby each new worker is attached to an experienced worker to learn. As a method it is held to have certain important advantages: it copes with the training of workers for highly specific jobs and for using the most up-to-date equipment; it is flexible as regards its timing; it can take place in all working places without disturbing the overall rhythm of production (Batyshev, 1971b:195). Its more serious drawbacks are that it gives the young worker little theoretical knowledge, it is limited to the use of one particular set of equipment and so cannot be a long-term method of training (Omel'yanenko, 1973:97-8). The experienced worker is required to teach the trainee how to use equipment and work accurately. In addition to imparting practical skills, his work contains an element of character education with respect to life in general and work in particular (Batyshev, 1971a:67). Individual training usually prepares workers for only the first grade of skill, but occasionally those who get good results are awarded a second grade.

Brigade training differs but little from individual training and the two are often bracketed together and discussed as 'the individual brigade method'. For production training the new worker is taught not in isolation but as part of a group of beginners formed into a 'study brigade' and supervised by a 'brigadier'. Brigade training accounted for 17.3 per cent of all workers trained on production in 1966 (Novgorodski and Khaykin, 1968:14).

The third method of training a new worker on the job is through *coursework*. In 1966, 11.5 per cent of workers trained on production were on such courses (Novgorodski and Khaykin, 1968:14). This method is used when the trade to be learnt requires a greater mastery of theoretical knowledge. Usually the courses are taken only by those who have complete secondary education, i.e. ten or eleven years of schooling (Orlovski, 1972:10). In recent years this method has become more widely used (1972:11) and government policy has stressed the importance of short courses as a training method (*Spravochnoe posobie po obucheniyu* . . .:15).

Whatever the form of training followed, two people assume a more important role in the training and activity of the factory than in the trade school. They are the tutor (*nastavnik*) and the master-craftsman. The tutor is an older worker who is assigned to a new apprentice to guide him through any work or moral problems he may encounter. In contrast to the master-craftsman, he is not relieved of his other work duties in order to teach. The tutorship movement is a relatively new campaign in Soviet labour training. (The Russian word for tutor is a revival of an old word marked 'obsolete' in the 1972 Oxford Russian-English Dictionary meaning 'mentor' or 'preceptor'. It is currently defined in the professional journal of vocational education as 'an older friend and teacher of youth'; *Professional'no-tekhnicheskoe obrazovanie,* December 1974:40.)

In the Kuznetsk metallurgical combine over 800 tutors are engaged to work with 1500 young workers. The brief of these tutors is to watch over the progress of the new workers, guide them into the trades where they fit best and help them to adapt to working life. It is estimated that the work of the tutors contributed to a 25.4 per cent reduction in the number of breaches of labour discipline among people under thirty in 1974 as compared with 1973 (*Metallurg,* November 1975:39-40).

The other major figure in the labour training of young workers on production is the master-craftsman. In the technical trade school he is only one of a large team in this area; in the factory he is the major person involved in the training of the young worker. Ideally he is both a skilled teacher and an experienced worker. It is repeatedly stressed, however, that the master-craftsman has an important character-educational role. He is called upon to instil a communist attitude in his pupils, a determination to overcome difficulties, a sense of collectivism and 'other qualities characterising the leading Soviet citizen' (Makienko *et al.,* 1971:127). It is his duty to observe systematically his pupils' success at work and attitudes to work; general development (ability with words, interest in books, other interests); behaviour; interest in social events and social attitudes; volitional qualities (determination, initiative, courage etc.); and material circumstances. These observations must not merely be mentally noted: they must also be written down along with the pupils' good and bad deeds, supposed reasons for these and the measures taken to handle each situation (Makienko *et al.*, 1971:129).

The tutors and master-craftsmen at the plant are not the only workers involved in educational work. The workers themselves are encouraged to take part in the guidance of local schoolchildren. The Cheropovets metallurgical plant, for instance, runs regular seminars for its workers who are involved in organising extra-curricular work in the schools. There are more than 900 members of these, of whom 80 per cent hold government awards and have been praised for their particularly high productivity. The seminars are organised by a plant council, which, along with the directors, the trade union, party and Komsomol committees, works out plans for additional vocational guidance, distributes awards to the best tutors and so on (*Metallurg*, November 1975:39-40).

SOVIET CRITICISM OF INITIAL FACTORY TRAINING

Factory training is criticised less in the educational press than is labour training in the technical trade schools, but this reflects the lower demands put on training on the job. As regards initial training, most factories can cope successfully with preparing workers for their own jobs and they are not usually expected to provide young workers with the skills for a wide variety of different conditions. If new expertise is later required, the worker is normally directed into one of the courses for retraining or for raising qualifications. Even within the fairly limited framework of training on the job, however, there are some problems reported in the press and these usually have a bearing on the people who act as teaching staff. It is calculated that in over 90 per cent of all factories the organisation of production training is the responsibility of only one or two workers (Pliner, 1970:21). They take all the basic decisions in their area, and there are no special regional organs for the guidance of production training. Frequently the links between evening schools and factory production centres are weak, and inadequate use is made of possibilities for co-operation. Perhaps the most common complaint concerning labour training on the job refers to the low calibre of the instructors. In 1964 in one district of Moscow it was estimated that 69 per cent of those involved in technical training on production did not have a higher education, and almost half of those had not even a complete secondary education (Pliner, 1970:21-2).

APPENDIX C
Changes in the Soviet Educational Stock over Time

	1914	1940	1960	1975
Population, at beginning of year, (1,000,000s)	159.2	194.1	212.4	255.5[b]
No. of pupils in 9th-10th (11th) classes (1000s)	102	1291	2597	10759
No. of students in vocational schools (1000s)	106	717	1141	3381
of whom in secondary technical trade schools	–	–	–	1216
of whom in technical schools	–	–	174	408
No. of students in secondary specialised schools (1000s)	54	975	2060	4525
No. of students in higher educational institutions (1000s)	127	812	2396	4854
No. of specialists with higher or secondary specialised education employed in the economy (1000s)	190[a]	2401	8784	22796
No. of people with complete higher education (1,000,000s)	–	1.2[d]	3.8[c]	11.9[b]
No. of people with secondary specialised education (1,000,000s)	–	–	7.9[c]	18.7[b]
No. of people with ten years' general education (1,000,000s)	–	–	9.9[c]	34.4[b]

[a] 1913
[b] 1976
[c] 1959
[d] 1939

Source: Narodnoe obrazovanie, nauka i kul'tura v SSSR Moscow 1977

Glossary of Russian Names and Terms

Gosbank   State bank

Gossnab   State committee on material supply

Gosplan   State planning commission

ITR   *(inzhenerno-tekhnicheski rabochi)* Literally, engineering-technical worker; a technician or engineer i.e. a worker performing tasks requiring higher or middle level qualifications and/or experience

Kollektiv   a group of people having a consciousness of working together and sharing similar social, political and economic interests

KP   *(Komsomol'ski Prozhektor)* Literally, 'Komsomol Searchlight'; komsomol agency of control in the factory, seeking to check on the quality of the work carried out

KPSS   *(Kommunisticheskaya Partiya Sovetskogo Soyuza)* Communist Party of the Soviet Union (CPSU)

MVSSO   *Ministerstvo Vysshego i Srednego Spetsial' nogo Obrazovaniya)* Ministry of Higher and Secondary Specialised Education

NOT   *(Nauchnaya Organizatsiya Truda)* Literally, Scientific Organisation of Labour; a much promoted Soviet concept urging the organisation of the work process in the most efficient way possible

NTO   *(Nauchno-Tekhnicheskoe Obshchestvo)* Literally, Scientific Technical Society; a club in a factory or school promoting scientific and technical interest

praktik   A person who has gained industrial skill through experience without any theoretic training

150

professiya Trade or occupation; 'the basic type of labour activity of a person in any branch of production, science, culture or consumer services. As examples can be given such well-known professions as metal-worker, turner, tractor-driver, engineer, agronomist, doctor, pedagogue, seamstress and so on' (Makienko *et al.*, 1971, p. 19). It can be seen that the concept is much broader than that of 'profession' in English.

PTU *(professional'no-tekhnicheskoe uchilishche)* A (vocational) technical trade school. Those offering a two-year course prepare students for a trade qualification; three-year courses give a general secondary education and trade training (SPTU)

VUZ *(vysshee uchebnoe zavedenie)* Higher educational institution

tarifny razryad Literally, tariff grade; an indicator of a worker's level of qualification and the complexity of his work. Most specialisms are divided into six grades

TU *(tekhnicheskoe uchilishche)* Technical school (one-year course)

VOIR *(Vsesoyuznoe Obshchestvo Izobretateley i Ratsionalizatorov)* Literally, All-Union Society of Inventors and Rationalisers; i.e. a movement within factories promoting innovatory and rationalising work among the entire workforce.

Bibliography

This bibliography contains all the works cited in the text plus other books relevant to the topics discussed.

ABSEES (quarterly journal of abstracts from the Soviet and East European press. Published by University of Glasgow), January 1970-January 1976.

AITOV, N.A. 'Izuchenie struktury rabochego klassa promyshlennogo tsentra', *Sotsiologicheskie issledovaniya*, 1/1974.

AITOV, N.A. 'Vliyanie obshcheobrazovatel'nogo urovnya rabochikh na ikh proizvodstvennuyu deyatel'nost', *Voprosy filosofii*, 11/1966.

ALEKSANDROV, N.A. *Dukhovny mir sovetskogo rabochego* (Moscow, 1975).

ANDRLE, V. 'Managerial Power in the Soviet Union: The Social Position of Industrial Directors' Ph.D.thesis, Birmingham University, 1975.

ANDRLE, V. *Managerial Power in the Soviet Union* (Lexington, Massachusetts, and Farnborough, Hampshire, 1976).

ANISIMOVA, Z. *Profgruppa: trud, byt, distsiplina* (Moscow, 1971).

ARUTYUNYAN, YU.V. 'Kollektivizatsiya sel'skogo khozyaystva i vysvobozhdenie rabochey sily dlya promyshlennosti', in *Formirovanie i razvitię sovetskogo rabochego klassa (1917-1961gg.)* (Moscow, 1964).

ASHMANE, M.E. 'Sotsial'ny sostav studenchestva Latviyskoy SSR' in *Sotsial'nye aspekty obrazovaniya* (Riga, 1972).

AVERICHEV, YU.P. 'On the Joint Work of General Education Schools and Vocational Technical Schools in Providing Vocational Guidance to Schoolchildren', *Soviet Education*, May 1972 (*Shkola i proizvodstvo*, 10/1971).

BATKAEVA, I.A. *Formy i sistemy zarabotnoy platy* (Moscow, 1973).

BATYSHEV, S.YA. *Formirovanie kvalifitsirovannykh rabochikh kadrov v SSSR* (Moscow, 1971a).

BATYSHEV, S.YA. *Osnovy proizvodstvennoy pedagogiki* (Moscow, 1971b).

BECKER, Howard. *Man in Reciprocity* (New York, 1956).

BERGSON, A. *The Structure of Soviet Wages: A Study in Socialist Economics* (Cambridge Massachusetts, 1944).

BERNSTEIN, B. 'On the Classification and Framing of Educational Knowledge', in E. Hopper, *Readings in the Theory of Educational Systems* (London, 1971).

BERNSTEIN, B. *Class, Codes and Control* (London, 1975).

BLAUNER, R. *Alienation and Freedom* (Chicago, 1964).

BLUMBERG, P. *Industrial Democracy: The Sociology of Participation* (London, 1968).

BLYAKHMAN, L.S., ZDRAVOMYSLOV, A.G., and SHKARATAN, O.I. *Dvizhenie rabochey sily na promyshlennykh predpriyatiyakh* (Moscow, 1965).

BLYAKHMAN, L.S. *et al. Podbor i rasstanovka kadrov na predpriyatii* (Moscow, 1968).

BLYAKHMAN, L.S. and SHKARATAN, O.I. *NTR, rabochi klass, intelligentsiya* (Moscow, 1973).

BOITER, A. 'When the Kettle Boils Over', *Problems of Communism*, 1/1964.

BORISOV, S.S. *Uchebno-vospitatel'naya rabota v Nizhne-Tagil'skom gorno-metallurgicheskom tekhnikume* (Moscow, 1974).
BORISOVA, L.V., PEN'KOV, E.I. and SEREGIN, A.S. 'Nekotorye rezul'taty sotsiologich-eskogo issledovaniya truda na promyshlennykh predpriyatiyakh Tul'skoy oblasti i Moskvy' in *Nauchnoe upravlenie obshchestvom* Vol. 2 (Moscow, 1968).
BRAVERMAN, H. *Labor and Monopoly Capital* (New York, 1974).
BRAZAYTIS, A. 'Postoyannaya nasha zabota', *Professional'no-tekhnicheskoe obrazovanie*, 1/1976.
BRODERSEN, Arvid, *The Soviet Worker* (New York, 1966).
BROWN, E.C. *Soviet Trade Unions and Labor Relations* (Cambridge, Massachusetts, 1966).
BULGAKOV, A.A. *Professional'no-tekhnicheskoe obrazovanie i profsoyuzy* (Moscow, 1973).
BULGAKOV, A.A. *Puti sovershenstvovaniya professional'no-tekhnicheskogo obrazovaniya v SSSR* (Moscow, 1976).
BULMER, Martin (ed.) *Working-Class Images of Society* (London, 1975).
BUNAKOV, A. 'Stanovlenie mastera', *Professional'no-tekhnicheskoe obrazovanie*, 1/1976.
BURNS, T. (ed.) *Industrial Man* (Harmondsworth, Middlesex, 1969).
Byulleten' Ministerstva Vysshego i Srednego Spetsial'nogo Obrazovaniya (referred to as *Byull. MVSSO*), March 1974.

CARY, CHARLES D. 'Peer Groups in the Political Socialisation of Soviet Children' *Social Science Quarterly*, 1974.
CASP (*Current Abstracts of the Soviet Press*).
CDSP (*Current Digest of the Soviet Press*).
CHAPMAN, J.G. *Real Wages in Soviet Russia since 1928* (Cambridge, Massachusetts, 1963).
CHAPMAN, J.G. *Wage Variations in Soviet Industry: The Impact of the 1956-1960 Wage Reform* (Santa Monica, California, 1970).
CHAPMAN, J.G. *Recent Trends in Soviet Industrial Wage Structure* (Washington: Kennan Institute, 1977).
CONNOR, W.D. *Deviance in Soviet Society: Crime, Delinquency and Alcoholism* (New York, 1972).
CONQUEST, R. *Industrial Workers in the USSR* (London, 1967).

DAGITE, I. *Iz opyta rukovodstva srednim spetsial'nym obrazovaniem v Litovskoy SSR* (Vilnius, 1973).
DARIBAEV, ZH. *Ekonomicheskoe obrazovanie i rost tvorcheskoy aktivnosti kollektiva* (Moscow, 1973).
DAYRI, N.G. 'Politekhnicheskoe obrazovanie, trudovoe vospitanie i prepodavanie istorii', *Sovetskaya pedagogika*, 3/1975.
Deyatel'nost' KPSS po razvitiyu sotsialisticheskoy kul'tury, Vol. 1 (Sverdlovsk, 1973).
DOBSON, R.B. 'Social Status and Inequality of Access to Higher Education'. In J. Karabel and A.H. Halsey, *Power and Ideology in Education* (New York, 1977).
DROZDOVA, O.P. 'Nekotorye problemy sotsial'nykh peremeshcheniy v ramkakh proizvodstvennogo ob'edineniya', in *Sovetskaya sotsiologicheskaya assotsiatsiya*, 1973.
DUNHAM, Vera S. *In Stalin's Time* (London, 1976).
D'YACHENKO, N.N. *Professional'naya orientatsiya i vovlochenie molodezhi v sistemu professional'no-tekhnicheskogo obrazovaniya* (Moscow, 1971).

ERSHOVA, E.A. *et al. Skorokhod* (Leningrad, 1969).
ETZIONI, A. *The Active Society* (New York, 1968).

FILIPPOV, F.R. *Sotsial'naya struktura obshchestva i sistema obrazovaniya* (Moscow, 1974).

FILIPPOV, F.R. 'Sotsial'nye peremeshcheniya v sovetskom obshchestve' *Sotsiologicheskie issledovaniya*, 4/1975.
Formirovanie i razvitie sovetskogo rabochego klassa (1917-1961gg.) (Moscow, 1964).

GARNSEY, E. 'Occupational Structure in Industrialised Societies', *Sociology*, vol. 9, no. 3, 1975.
GITELMAN, Z. 'Soviet Political Culture: Insights from Jewish Emigres' *Soviet Studies*, vol. 29, no. 4. October 1977.
GOL'DSHTEYN, E.N. 'Promyshlennoye predpriyatie i obrazovanie rabochikh', in *Deyatel'nost' KPSS po razvitiyu sotsialisticheskoy kul'tury*, vol. 1 (Sverdlovsk, 1973).
GONCHAROV, N.F. *Kommunisticheskoe vospitanie rabochikh promyshlennykh predpriyatiy* (Voronezh, 1972).
GORDON, L. and KLOPOV, E. *Sotsial'noe razvitie rabochege klassa* (Moscow, 1974).
GRANT, N. *Soviet Education* (Harmondsworth, Middlesex, 1972). .
GUROVA, R.G. (ed.) *Sotsiologicheskie problemy obrazovaniya i vospitaniya* (Moscow, 1973).
GUR'YANOV, S.T. and SEKRETARYUK, V.V. *Prizvanie i professiya* (Moscow, 1974).

HABERMAS, J. *Legitimation Crisis* (London, 1976).
HALSEY, A.H. *et al. Education, Economy and Society* (New York, 1961).
HANS, N. *The Russian Tradition in Education* (London, 1963).
HOLLANDER, P. *Soviet and American Society: A Comparison* (New York, 1973).
HOLUBENKO, M. 'The Soviet Working Class', *Critique*, no. 4, Spring 1975.
HOPPER, E. *Readings in the Theory of Educational Systems* (London, 1971)
HORDLEY, I. and LEE, D.J. 'Social Change in Technical Education' *Sociology*, vol. 4, no. 1, 1970.
HOUGH, J.F. 'Political Participation in the Soviet Union', *Soviet Studies* vol. 38, no. 1, 1976.

IL'YASOV, SH.Z. *Trudyashchiesya v upravlenii proizvodstvom* (Makhachkala, 1971).
IOVCHUK, M.T. and KOGAN, L.N. (eds.) *Dukhovny mir sovetskogo rabochego* (Moscow, 1972a).
IOVCHUK, M.T. and KOGAN, L.N. *Pod''em kul'turno-tekhnicheskogo urovnya sovetskogo rabochego klassa* (Moscow, 1972b).
Itogi vsesoyuznoy perepisi naseleniya 1970g, vol. 6 (Moscow, 1973).
IVANOV, A.I. 'Slushatel' podgotovitel'nogo otdeleniya i ego motivizatsiya vysshego obrazovaniya', in *Sotsial'nye aspekty obrazovaniya* (Riga, 1972).
IVANOV, S.I. and TSURKANU, N.V. 'Sotsial'nye aspekty agrarno-promyshlennoy integratii' *Sotsiologicheskie issledovaniya*, 2/1975.
IVANOVICH, K.A. and EPSHTEYN, D.A. (eds) *Pedagogicheskie osnovy trudovogo obucheniya v obshcheobrazovatel'noy shkole* (Moscow, (1968)
IVANOVICH, K.A. and EPSHTEYN, D.A. *Trudovoe politekhnicheskoe obuchenie v sredney shkole* (Moscow, 1972).
IVASHKEVICH, V. *Glavnoe napravlenie* (Kiev, 1975).
Izvestiya 25 May 1958; 22 July 1967; 16 April 1968; 7 July 1971; 23 July 1971; 10 August 1971; 3 September 1972; 7 November 1973; 9 May 1974; 15 May 1974; 26 May 1974; 22 September 1974; 5 April 1975.

KAPLAN, I.I. 'The Influence of Education on Labor Output', in D. Noah (ed.), *The Economics of Education in the USSR* (New York, 1969).
KASHIN, M.P. and CHEKARIN, E.M. (eds). *Narodnoe obrazovanie v RSFSR* (Moscow, 1970).
KAYDALOV, D.P. and SUYMENKO, E.I. *Aktual'nye problemy sotsiologii truda* (Moscow, 1974).

KHAIKIN, N.M. 'Technical-Economic Indexes of the Labor of Workers with Different Vocational Preparation', in D. Noah (ed.), *The Economics of Education in the USSR* (New York, 1969).

Khimicheskaya promyshlennost' (journal of the chemical industry, Moscow), 9/1975.

KINKADZE, T.V. *Professional'nye izmeneniya v sostave rabochikh kadrov Rustavskogo metallurgicheskogo zavoda* (Tbilisi, 1973).

KIRSCH, J.L. *Soviet Wages: Changes in Structures and Administration since 1956* (Boston, 1972).

KISSEL', A.A. 'Uroven' obrazovaniya rabochego i otnoshenie k trudu', in A.G. Zdravomyslov and V.A. Yadov, *Trud i razvitie lichnosti* (Leningrad, 1965).

KOKIN, YU. P. *Zarabotnaya plata i istochniki ee rosta, pri sotsializme* (Moscow, 1974).

KOMAROV, V.E. 'The Efficiency of Day, Correspondence and Evening Education' in D. Noah (ed.), *The Economics of Education in the USSR* (New York, 1969).

KOMAROV, V.E. *Ekonomicheskie problemy podgotovki i ispol'zovaniya kadrov spetsialistov* (Moscow, 1972).

Kommunist, no. 17, 1965; no. 15, 1967. No. 16, 1976.

Komsomol'skaya pravda 2 June 1967; 29 November 1968; 29 September 1969; 25 August 1972; 16 March 1973; 27 October 1973; 30 October 1973; 28 September 1974; 30 October 1974; 23 August 1977.

KONONENKO, B.I. *Rol' professional'noy orientatsii v kommunisticheskom vospitanii molodezhi* (avtoreferat) (Tashkent, 1972).

KOVALENKO, A. 'Detishche zavoda', *Professional'no-tekhnicheskoe obrazovanie*, 1/1976.

KOZHAMKULOV, T. *Podgotovka kvalifikatsionnykh rabochikh kadrov v Kazakhstane* (Alma-Ata, 1972).

KOZYREV, YU.N. 'Potrebnost' naseleniya v vysshem obrazovanii i otbor molodezhi v vuzy', in *Molodezh' i obrazovanie* (Moscow, 1972).

'KPSS v tsifrakh', *Partiinaya zhizn'*, no. 10, May 1976.

KRAVTSOV, N.I. *Soderzhanie metodicheskoy raboty v sisteme professional'no-tekhnicheskogo obrazovaniya* (Moscow, 1974).

KREVNEVICH, V.V. *Vliyanie nauchno-tekhnicheskogo progressa na izmenenie struktury rabochego klassa SSSR* (Moscow, 1971).

KRYLOV, A.A. and IVANOVA, L.S. 'Predvaritel'nye itogi eksperimental'noy proverki uchebnogo plana proftekhuchilishch shveynikov, podgotavlivayushchikh kvalifitsirovannykh rabochikh so srednim obrazovaniem', *VNII professional'no-tekhnicheskogo obrazovaniya. Nauchno-tekhnicheski sbornik*, vol. 30 (Leningrad, 1972).

KRYLOV, N.I. 'Professional'naya orientatsiya uchashcheysya molodezhi kak problema nravstvennogo vospitaniya', *Voprosy psikhologii*, 1/1973.

KSENOFONTOVA, V.V. *Zhiznennye plany shkol'noy molodezhi i ikh realizatsiya* (avtoreferat) (Sverdlovsk, 1972).

KUGEL, S.A. and NIKANDROV, O.A. *Molodye inzhenery* (Moscow, 1971 — extracts also translated in *Soviet Education*, May 1972).

KULAGIN, G. 'Kto zavtra vstanet k stanku?' *Nash sovremennik*, 11/1974a; 12/1974b.

KUZ'MIN, B.A. *Tekhnikumy i uchilishcha SSSR* (Moscow, 1974).

KUZNETSOV, E.M. *Politicheskaya agitatsiya* (Moscow, 1974).

Labour Focus on Eastern Europe, vol. 2, no. 1, 1978.

LANE, D.S. *The Roots of Russian Communism* (London, 1969; reprinted 1974).

LANE, D.S. *The End of Inequality? Stratification under State Socialism* (Harmondsworth, Middlesex, 1971).

LANE, D.S. 'Marxist Class Conflict Analyses of State Socialist Society' in R. Scase, *Industrial Society: Class, Cleavage and Control* (London, 1977).

LANE, D.S. *Politics and Society in the USSR* (London, second edition 1978).

LEBEDEVA, N.B. and SHKARATAN, O.I. *Ocherki istorii sotsialisticheskogo sorevnovaniya* (Leningrad, 1966).

LENIN, V.I. 'Razvitie kapitalizma v Rossii'. *Polnoe sobranie sochineniy* (referred to as *PSS*) vol. 3, 1958.

LEVIKOV, A. *Pimeny XX veka* (Moscow, 1973).

LEVIN, B. 'Three Cautionary Tales for the Admirers of the Great Workers' State'. *The Times* (London), 28 December 1977.

LIFEROV, L.A. and DOBRUSIN, D.L. *Obuchenie i vospitanie na zanyatiyakh v shkol'nykh masterskikh* (Moscow, 1969).

LISOVSKI, V.T. and DMITRIEV, A.V. *Lichnost' studenta* (Leningrad, 1974).

LOCKWOOD, D. 'Sources of Variation in Working-class Images of Society', *Sociological Review*, vol. 14, 1966; reprinted in M. Bulmer, *Working-Class Images of Society* (London, 1975).

LOZAREV, A.S. and KAZAKOVA, YU.P. *Ob opyte raboty partkoma zavoda 'Dvigatel' ' po sozdaniyu plana sotsial'nogo razvitiya* (Tallin, 1971).

LYKOVA, L. 'Dlya zhenshchin strany Sovetov', *Trud*, no. 152, 1 July 1977.

MCAULEY, MARY *Labour Disputes in Soviet Russia 1957-1965* (Oxford, 1969).

MCKENZIE, R.T. and SILVER, A. *Angels in Marble: Working-class Conservatives in Urban England* (London, 1968).

MAKIENKO, N.I. *et al. Pedagogicheski protsess v uchebnykh zavedeniyakh professional'no-tekhnicheskogo obrazovaniya* (Minsk, 1971).

MALAKHOVA, L.K. *Rost professional'no-tekhnicheshogo urovnya zhenshchin-rabotnits v period semiletki (1959-1968)* (avtoreferat) (Moscow, 1971).

MANGUNOV, I.S. *Inzhener: Sotsiologo-ekonomicheski ocherk* (Moscow, 1973).

MATRAS, Judah, *Populations and Societies* (Chicago, 1970).

MATTHEWS, M. *Class and Society in Soviet Russia* (London, 1972).

MATTHEWS, M. 'Top Incomes in the USSR: Towards a Definition of the Soviet Elite' *Survey*, Summer 1975.

Metallurg (journal of the metallurgical industry, Moscow) 9/1975; 10/1975; 11/1975; 12;1975.

Metodicheskie rekomendatsii po povysheniyu effektivnosti uchebnogo protsessa v tekhnicheskikh uchilishchakh (Moscow, 1973).

Molodezh' i obrazovanie (Moscow, 1972).

Molodoy kommunist, 2/1962.

Moskovski stankostroitel'ny zavod im. Sergo Ordzhonikidze (Moscow, 1975).

MUKHACHEV, V.I. and BOROVIK, V.S. *Rabochi klass i upravlenie proizvodstvom* (Moscow, 1975).

MYAKSHINA, K. 'Rabochie universitety', *Sotsialisticheskaya industriya* no. 75, 30 March 1976.

Narkhoz 1922-1972gg. (Moscow, 1972).

Narkhoz [abbreviation for *Narodnoe khozyaystro SSSR*] *1974* (Moscow, 1975).

Narkhoz 1975 (Moscow, 1976).

Narkhoz za 60 let (Moscow, 1977).

Narodnoe obrazovanie, November 1969.

Narodnoe upravlenie proizvodstvom, vol. 2 (Moscow, 1968).

Nauchnoe upravlenie obshchestvom, vol. 2 (Moscow, 1968).

NOAH, D. (ed.) *The Economics of Education in the USSR* (New York, 1969).

NOR', A.V. *et al.* 'Nauchno-tekhnicheskaya revolyutsiya i nekotorye voprosy podgotovki i povysheniya kvalifikatsii rabochikh kadrov i ITR', *Uchenye zapiski kafedr politicheskoy ekonomiki vysshikh partiynykh shkol,* vol. 11 (1972), pp. 138-63.

NOVE, A. 'Is there a Ruling Class in the USSR?', *Soviet Studies*, vol. 27, 4/1975.
NOVGORODSKI, YU.F. and KHAYKIN, N.M. *Podgotovka kadrov dlya promyshlennosti* (Moscow, 1968).
NOVIKOVA, T.M. 'Obshchestvennaya rabota v strukture byudzheta vremeni partiynykh aktivistov', *Sotsiologicheskie issledovaniya*, 1/1976.

O'DELL, F. 'Soviet Child Socialisation: Children's Literature, a Case Study' Ph.D. thesis, University of Birmingham, 1975.
OFER, G. *The Service Sector in Soviet Economic Growth* (Cambridge, Massachusetts, 1973).
OL'SHANSKI, V.B. 'Lichnost' i sotsial'nye tsennosti', in *Sotsiologiya v SSSR*, vol. 1 (Moscow, 1965).
OMEL'YANENKO, B.L. *Tekhnicheski progress i sovremennye trebovaniya k urovnyu kvalifikatsii i podgotovka rabochikh kadrov* (Moscow, 1973).
Opyt raboty profsoyuznoy gruppy tkatskogo proizvodstva Gus'-Khrustal'nogo tekstil'nogo kombinata Vladimirskoy oblasti, odobrenny Presidiumom VTsSPS (Vladimir, 1970).
ORLOVSKI, YU.P. *Spravochnik molodogo rabochego.* Moscow, 1972.
OSIPOV, G.V. (ed.) *Industry and Labour in the USSR* (London, 1966).
OSIPOV, V.I. *Sotsial'noe razvitie rabochego klassa v usloviyakh nauchno-tekhnicheskoy revolyutsii* (Saratov, 1975).
OSTROUMOV, 'Prestupnost' i ego prichiny', in *Nauka i zhizn'*, no. 7, 1968.

Partiya i rabochi klass v usloviyakh stroitel'stva kommunizma (Moscow, 1973).
Partiinaya zhizn', 10/1976.
Partiinaya zhizn', 21/1977.
Pedagogicheskaya entsiklopediya, 4 vols. (Moscow, 1964-68).
PERMAN, Z.A. *Ob opyte raboty ob"edinennogo postroykoma tresta 'Kemerovokhimstroy' po rasprostraneniyu i razvitiyu pochina brigady N.P. Zhdanova 'vypol'nit' pyatiletnee zadanie v fizicheskikh ob"emakh v 3.5 godakh'* (Kemerovo, 1974).
Perspektivnoe planirovanie vospitatel'noy raboty v srednem proftekhuchilishche (Riga, 1974).
PETROV, YU. and FILIPPOV, F. *Kak stanovyatsya rabochimi* (Sverdlovsk, 1973).
PLINER, M.D. 'Nekotorye sotsial'no-ekonomicheskie problemy podgotovki i povysheniya kul'turno-tekhnicheskogo urovnya rabochikh na predpriyatii', *VNII Professional'no-tekhnicheskogo obrazovaniya. Uchenye zapiski* vol. 1 (Leningrad, 1970).
PLINER, M.D. and INOSTRANTSEV, A.V. 'Sotsial'no-ekonomicheskie faktory sozdaniya srednikh proftekhuchilishch', *VNII Professional'no-tekhnicheskogo obrazovaniya. Nauchnye trudy*, vol. 5 (Leningrad, 1974).
PODOROV, G.M. 'Opyt sotsiologicheskikh issledovaniy trudovoy distsipliny na predpriyatiyakh Gor'kovskoy oblasti', *Sotsiologicheskie issledovaniya*, 4/1976.
POULANTZAS, N. *Class in Contemporary Capitalism* (London, 1975).
Pravda, 29 June 1966; 27 January 1968; 18 June 1971; 6 March 1974; 27 May 1974; 16 March 1975; 25 March 1975; 19 September 1976.
Pravovoe polozhenie professional'nykh soyuzov SSSR (Leningrad, 1962).
Problemy proforientatsii i profotbora (Kiev, 1974).
Professional'no-tekhnicheskoe obrazovanie (referred to as *Prof-tekh.obr.*), 12/1974.
Profsoyuzy SSSR: Dokumenty i materialy 1963-1973gg. Vol. 5 (Moscow, 1974).
Programma sredney shkoly: trudovoe obuchenie: Avtodelo (Moscow, 1971).
Programmy fakul'tativnykh kursov (Moscow, 1972).
Programmy vos'miletney shkoly: nachal'nye klassy (Moscow, 1971).

Rabochi klass razvitogo sotsialisticheskogo obshchestva (Moscow, 1974).

158   *The Soviet Industrial Worker*

Radio Liberty Research. RL 250/77, Munich, 31 October 1977. RL 24/78, Munich, 1 February 1978.

RASHIN, A.G. 'Rost kul'turno-tekhnicheskogo urovnya rabochego klassa SSSR v 1917-58gg.', *Istoriya SSSR*, no. 2, March-April 1961.

ROZANOV, M.D. *Obukhodtsy* (Leningrad, 1965).

RUBLE, B.A. 'The Role of the Factory Trade-Union Committee in Defense of Workers' Legal Rights', (Washington: Kennan Institute, 1977).

RUTKEVICH, M.N. and FILIPPOV, F.R. *Sotsial'nye peremeshcheniya* (Moscow, 1970).

RUTKEVICH, M.N. and FILIPPOV, F.R. 'Principles of the Marxist Approach to Social Structure and Social Mobility', in M. Yanowitch and W.A. Fisher (eds) *Social Stratification and Social Mobility in the USSR* (New York, 1973).

RUTKEVICH, M.N. and SENYAIKOVA, L.I. 'O sotsial'nom sostava studenthestva v SSSR i tendentsiyakh ego izmeneniya' in *Sotsial'nye razlichiya i ikh preodolenie* (Sverdlovsk, 1969).

SCHROEDER, G.E. 'An Appraisal of Soviet Wage and Income Statistics', in G.P. Treml and J.P. Hardt (eds) (Durham, North Carolina, 1972).

SENYAVSKI, S.L. *et al. Rabochi klass SSSR, 1938-1965gg.* (Moscow, 1971).

SHAFRANOVA, O.I. *Professional'ny sostav rabochikh promyshlennosti SSSR* (Moscow, 1972).

SHANTRUKOVA, L. 'Ekzamen na zrelost', *Professional'no-tekhnicheskoe obrazovanie*, 12/1974.

SHIRINSKI, V.I. 'O gotovnosti vypusknikov shkoly k trudu v sfere promyshlennogo proizvodstva' in R.G. Gurova (ed.), *Sotsiologicheskie problemy obrazovaniya i vospitaniya* (Moscow, 1973).

SHIROBOKOV, A. 'Sfera komsomol'skogo deystviya', *Professional'no-tekhnicheskoe obrazovanie*, 12/1975.

SHKARATAN, O.I. 'Sotsial'naya struktura sovetskogo rabochego klassa', *Voprosy filosofii*, 1/1967.

SHKARATAN, O.I. *Problemy sotsial'noy struktury rabochego klassa SSSR* (Moscow, 1970). *Shkola i proizvodstvo*, 1/1971.

SHLAPAK, N.A. *Zhiznennye plany vypusknikov sel'skikh shkol i ikh realizatsiya* (avtoreferat) (Sverdlovsk, 1967).

SHUBANOV, V. 'Mesto v zhizni', *Molodoy kommunist*, 6/1971.

SHUBKIN, V.N. 'Molodezh' vstupaet v zhizn', *Voprosy filosofii*, 5/1965.

SHUBKIN, V.N. *Sotsiologicheskie opyty* (Moscow, 1970).

SHUBKIN, V.N. 'Professiya—problema vybora', in *Nauka i zhizn'*, 5/1975; 10/1971.

SMOLYARCHUK, V. *Prava profsoyuzov v regulirovanii trudovykh otnosheniy rabochikh i sluzhashchikh* (Moscow, 1973).

SOKOL'NIKOV, Yu. L. 'Sotsialisticheskaya distsiplina truda i puti ee ulushcheniya', *Sotsiologicheskie issledovaniya*, 1/1976.

SONIN, M. *Izmeneniya professional'no-kvalifikatsionnoy struktury zhenskogo truda i sem'ya* (Moscow, 1972).

Sotsialisticheski trud, 1/1969.

Sotsial'nye aspekty obrazovaniya (Riga, 1972).

Sotsial'nye razlichiya i ikh preodolenie (Sverdlovsk, 1969).

Sovetskaya sotsiologicheskaya assotsiatsiya (Moscow, 1973).

Sovetskoe gosudarstvo i pravo, 8/1968.

The Soviet Union 1974-1975 (London, 1976).

SPASIBENKO, S.G. 'Labor Productivity and Worker Qualifications' in D. Noah (ed.) *The Economics of Education in the USSR* (New York, 1969).

Spravochnoe posobie po obucheniyu rabochikh kadrov na proizvodstve (Moscow, 1970; 1975).

Srednee spetsial'noe obrazovanie.

SSR v tsifrakh v 1976g. (Moscow, 1977).
Strana sovetov za 50 let (Moscow, 1968).
STRUMILIN, S.G. *Khozyaystvennoe znachenie narodnogo obrazovaniya* (Moscow-Leningrad, 1924).
STRUMILIN, S.G. *Problemy ekonomiki truda* (Moscow, 1957).

TAUKIN, B.P. and NOVIKOV, V.D. *Kontrol' deyatel'nosti administratsii* (Leningrad, 1974).
TECKENBERG, W. 'Labour Turnover and Job Satisfaction', *Soviet Studies*, vol. 30, no. 2, 1978.
'Tekhnicheskoe uchilishche: problemy i suzhdeniya' *Professional'no-tekhnicheskoe obrazovanie*, 1/1976.
THERBORN, G. *Science, Class and Society* (London, 1976).
TICKTIN, H. 'The Contradictions of Soviet Society and Professor Bettelheim', *Critique*, no. 6, Spring 1976.
The Times (London), 27 January 1978.
Tipovye uchebnye programmy dlya rabotnikov promyshlennosti i drugikh otrasley (Moscow, 1974).
Tipovye uchebnye programmy po novym kursam na 1975-76 uchebny god dlya rabotnikov promyshlennosti i drugikh otrasley (Moscow, 1975).
TITMA, M.KH. 'Tsennosti vliyayushchie na vybor professii', *Voprosy filosofii*, 4/1969.
TITMA, M.KH. *Sotsial'no-professional'naya orientatsiya uchashcheysya molodezhi* (avtoreferat) (Moscow, 1974).
TKACH, M. 'Career Plans of Graduates of Complete Secondary Schools', in M.N. Rutkevich, *The Career Plans of Youth* (New York, 1969).
TÖKES, R.L. (ed.) *Dissent in the USSR: Politics, Ideology and People* (Baltimore, 1975).
TREIMAN, D. 'Industrialisation and Social Stratification', *Sociological Inquiry*, no. 40, Spring 1970.
TREML, V.G. and HARDT, J.P. (eds) *Soviet Economic Statistics* (Durham, North Carolina 1972).
Trud, 30 June 1974.
TSATSKO, T. 'Vospityvat' traditsii', *Professional'no-tekhnicheskoe obrazovanie*, 12/1975.
Tsvetnye metally (journal of the non-ferrous metals industry, Moscow), 1/1976.
TUNDYKOV, YU.N. 'Znanie kak predposylka formirovaniya nravstvennoy lichnosti' in *Dukhovnoe razvitie lichnosti* (Sverdlovsk, 1967).
TUNDYKOV, YU.N. 'O sotsial'noy obuslovlennosti urovnya nravstvennogo soznaniya nekotorykh sloev rabochey molodezhi', in *Sotsial'nye razlichiya i ikh preodolenie* (Sverdlovsk, 1969).
TURCHENKO, V.N. *Nauchno-tekhnicheskaya revolyutsiya i revolyutsiya v obrazovanii* (Moscow, 1973).
TURNER, R.H. 'Models of Social Ascent through Education: Sponsored and Contest Mobility', in A.H. Halsey *et al., Education, Economy and Society* (New York, 1961).
TYAZHELNIKOV, E.M. 'Sovetskaya molodezh' i nauchno-tekhnicheski progress', *Kommunist*, 16/1971.

Uchitel'skaya gazeta (newspaper for teachers), 11 January 1964.

VASIL'EV, M.I. *et al. Sestroretski instrumental'ny zavod im. Voskova* (Leningrad, 1968).
VASIL'EVA, E.K. *Sotsial'no-professional'ny uroven' gorodskoy molodezhi* (Leningrad, 1973).
Vestnik statistiki. 1/1971.
VNII professional'no-tekhnicheskogo obrazovaniya. Nauchno-tekhnicheski sbornik, vol. 30 (Leningrad, 1972).

VNII professional'no-tekhnicheskogo obrazovaniya. Nauchnye trudy, vol. 5 (Leningrad, 1965); vol. 5 (1974).

VNII professional'no-tekhnicheskogo obrazovaniya. Uchenye zapiski, vol. 1 (Leningrad, 1970).

VODZINSKAYA, V.V. 'Otnoshenie molodogo rabochego k svoey professii', in A.G. Zdravomyslov and V.A. Yadov, *Trud i razvitie lichnosti* (Leningrad, 1965).

VODZINSKAYA, V.V. 'Orientations to Occupations', in M. Yanowitch and W.A. Fisher, *Social Stratification and Mobility in the USSR* (New York, 1973).

Voprosy psikhologii, 1/1973.

Vsesoyuznoe soveshchanie rabotnikov srednego spetsial'nogo obrazovaniya v Moskve 25-27 fevralya 1975 goda (Moscow, 1975).

WESTERGAARD, J.H. 'Radical Class Consciousness: A Comment', in M. Bulmer (ed.), *Working-Class Images of Society* (London, 1975).

WHITE, S. 'The USSR: Patterns of Autocracy and Industrialism', cyclostyled paper, University of Glasgow, 1975.

WILES, P. 'Recent Data on Soviet Income Distribution', *Survey*, Summer 1975.

WRIGHT, E.O. 'Class Boundaries in Advanced Capitalist Societies', *New Left Review*, no. 98, July/August 1976.

YANOWITCH, M. and FISHER, W.A. *Social Stratification and Mobility in the USSR* (New York, 1973).

YINGER, J. MILTON. 'Contraculture and subculture', *American Sociological Review*, vol. 25, 1960.

ZBOROVSKI, G.E. and ORLOV, G.P. *Dosug: Deystvitel'nost' i illyuzii* (Sverdlovsk, 1970).

ZDRAVOMYSLOV, A.G. and YADOV, V.A. *Trud i razvitie lichnosti* (Leningrad, 1965).

ZDRAVOMYSLOV, A.G. and YADOV, V.A. 'Effect of Vocational Distinctions on Attitudes to Work', in G.V. Osipov, *Industry and Labour in the USSR* (London, 1966).

ZDRAVOMYSLOV, A.G., ROZHIN, V.P. and YADOV, V.A. (eds) *Chelovek i ego rabota* (Moscow, 1967; translated *Man and his Work*, White Plains, New York, 1970).

ZHAMIN, V.A. 'Contemporary Problems of the Economics of Education', in D. Noah, *The Economics of Education in the USSR* (New York, 1969).

Zhenshchiny v SSSR (Moscow, 1975).

'Zhenshchiny v SSSR; statisticheskie materialy', *Vestnik statistiki*, 1/1971.

ZHOLKOV, A. 'Premiya'. *Sotsialisticheskaya industriya*, no. 29, 5 February 1976.

ZHURAVLEV, V.V. and GOL'DIN, L.G. 'Povysshenie kvalifikatsii i effektivnost' truda rukovoditeley i spetsialistov', *Khimicheskaya promyshlennost'*, 1/1976.

ZHURAVLEVA, G.A. 'Nekotorye voprosy vuzovskoy orientatsii molodezhi', in *Molodezh' i obrazovanie* (Moscow, 1972).

ZOTOVA, O.I., ASHKINAZI, A.G. and KOVALENKO, YU. P. *O nekotorykh sotsiologicheskikh aspektakh vybora professii vypusknikami srednikh shkol* (Moscow, 1970).

Index

Absenteeism 70−1
Achievement 59−60, 61, 87
Administration of Soviet factory 22
Administrative workers 106
Agriculture, men occupied in 12
Aitov N.A. on: educational background and job satisfaction 43; pupils' job choice 74−6; wages for monotonous work 87
Alcoholism 72−3
Alienation 40−2, 44, 45
All-Union Society of Inventors and Rationalisers (VOIR) 33
Alternative route 93, 97−105
Ambition 54, 60, 93, 106, 134
Andrle V. on: power of Party secretary 25; career patterns of factory directors 124−5
Anisimova Z. on: links between management and shop floor 23; trade union at workshop level 30−1; trade union role in private life 31
Arutyunyan Yu. V. on: urbanisation of population 8
Ashmane M.E. on: social background of students in Latvian higher education 101, 116
Aspirations 112−6, 119; of girls 118; by gender 130
Attestation Committee 24−6

Batkaeva I.A. on: wage structure in industry 80−1, 82
Batyshev S. Ya. on: need for vocational guidance 96; on-the-job training 146
Becker H. on: semi-socialised personality type 73
Bernstein B. on: education and social control 53
Bias in research in the USSR 1−2
Blauner R. on: alienation 41
Blyakhman L.S. and Shkaratan O.I. on: career patterns of factory directors 123−4; career patterns of workers occupying positions of authority 124−5; educational background of managerial workers 122; educational progress and social background 102; status of higher education 90
Blyakhman L.S. on: educational background of Leningrad workers 10
Blumberg P. on: relationships to means of production 44
Boiter A. on: strikes 48
Bonus 37, 80−1
Borisov S.S. on: teaching schedules at the PTU 140
Borisova L.V. on: labour discipline 71−2
Borovik V.S. see Mukhachev
Braverman H. 5 on: division of labour in East and West 15−6
Brigades 56
Brigade-leaders 23
Brigade-training 146
Bronfenbrenner U. on: effectiveness of political education 49
Brown E.C. on: career patterns of factory directors 123; resolution of worker disputes 51; troubles at work 48
Bulgakov A. on: propaganda for PTUs 87
Bureaucracy 135
Bureaucratic structures 38

Campaigns 25−6
Capital 40
Career paths 123−5
Cash nexus 49
Chapman J.G. on: growth in labour productivity 14; Khrushchev's wage reforms 80; wage structure in modern industry 82
Class 44; boundaries 6; consciousness 5, 49, 50−1, 136; exploitation 136; for itself 3, 41, 136; interests 5; and managerial groups 5
Clubs and unions 29
Collective farmers 3−4, 114
Collectivism 57
Commissions, at factory 28

161